JOSEPH CONRAD:

HIS ROMANTIC-REALISM

JOSEPH CONRAD

HIS ROMANTIC-REALISM

BY

RUTH M. STAUFFER

HASKELL HOUSE PUBLISHERS LTD.

Publishers of Scarce Scholarly Books

NEW YORK, N. Y. 10012

1969

First Published 1922

HASKELL HOUSE PUBLISHERS Ltd.
Publishers of Scarce Scholarly Books
280 LAFAYETTE STREET
NEW YORK, N. Y. 10012

Library of Congress Catalog Card Number: **67-31291**

Standard Book Number 8383-0794-9

TO

LETTIE ETHEL STEWART

TABLE OF CONTENTS

JOSEPH CONRAD:

HIS ROMANTIC-REALISM

PART I

THE MEANING OF ROMANTIC-REALISM AND ITS
APPLICATION TO CONRAD

LITERARY formulas are in themselves dead leaves blown here and there before the breath of many critics. Vital once, and full of color, they come too soon to be mere dried skeletons animated only by passing winds of contention until there arises the man who can quicken them to new birth. "Realism, Romanticism, Naturalism, even the unofficial sentimenalism" through the medium of "the old, old words, worn thin, defaced by ages of careless usage" become recreated when a new artist,— whether he be writer of verse or of prose matters little,— has given the world once more to see "the truth of life." Such is the genius of Joseph Conrad.

Now after Conrad's twenty-six years of literary activity, critics are practically unanimous in granting him a place in the highest rank of novelists. Galsworthy's tribute in 1908 when *The Secret Agent* had added the tenth to the list of Conrad's published works, has become one of the best know critical dicta of the decade: "The writing of these ten books," he said, "is probably the only writing of the last twelve years that will enrich the English language." Ford Hueffer goes so far as to declare, "Literature and Conrad are to me interchangeable terms." Mr. J. M. Robertson begins an article on Conrad in the *North American Review* of September, 1918, with the statement: "Conrad, I suppose, would by a vote of literary men be generally given the highest place in fiction in our day." No less enthusiastic is the estimate placed upon Joseph Conrad's work by the foremost critics in England, America, and France.

Yet in spite of the high esteem in which all thoughtful critics hold him, these same men are puzzled to know how to pigeon-hole him. They acclaim his distinction, his originality, but they disagree among themselves whether he is to be labeled Realist or Romanticist. William Lyon Phelps decides: "Now, there is nothing romantic about Conrad except his medium—the sea." Gilbert de Voisins in one of the most recent articles on Conrad asks: "D où vient donc cette accusation de réalism excessif qui l'a si longtemps poursuivi et qu' il retrouvait sous la plume de tant de critiques?" At one of these two extremes many critics range themselves.

There are those, however, who see in Conrad's work a union of these two schools that swayed the literature of the past century. Mr. Richard Curle, Conrad's official biographer, says in his book, *Joseph Conrad: A Study*: "It is indeed strangely appropriate that the man who has led one of the most wandering and one of the hardest lives of our time should have written the most realistically-romantic novels of our age."

When we come to examine the meanings that have accrued to these two terms in the course of literary debate, we conclude that in Conrad's work the emphasis seems to lie the other way: he is rather a Romantic-Realist than a writer of "realistically-romantic novels,"—or, better still, there is almost equal balance between the two. Joseph Conrad employs Realism or Romanticism or both whenever either or both may be needed to create the impression of actuality. In fact, Mr. Curle himself in the latter part of his book reverses his own emphasis. He says in Chapter XI, "I do not think I am exaggerating when I say that Conrad ranks with the great romantic realists of modern times," and again, "For it is as a realist that Conrad is most impressive . . . The spirit of his work is realistic in a rare and curious manner. For it is a realism which includes romance as one of its chief assets." One of the best brief discussions of the Romantic-Realism of Conrad's art appears in the little volume on Conrad by Hugh Walpole. The Folletts have summarized the secret of Joseph Conrad's originality and power in an article on his work that was published in the Alantic Monthly in 1917:

"If Mr. Joseph Conrad appears at first glimpse as a romancer,—and it is certain to many readers he does,—the explanation is simply that he is a deeper realist than is commonly perceived."

What is Romanticism? What is Realism? The mind of the world is perpetually demanding exact definitions of all abstractions. It would be wearisome even to enumerate the books and essays that have been written in all languages to define these two terms. A full examination of every one of these is out of place here. Each

critic has chosen some definite phase as the differentiating
factor between Romanticism and Realism.   But a study
of the work of the artists themselves, who are creating,
not defining, will reveal that the distinctions underlying
the Romantic and the Realistic are of three kinds: a
difference in subject matter; a difference in method; and
lastly, a difference in the spirit of the writer.*

Literary tradition has come to accept certain events
and circumstances in life as pertaining wholly to the
province of the Romantic writer, and it has decreed
that they are as rigorously to be shunned by the Realist.

Romance, in the first place, deals with the unfamiliar.
To satisfy this love of the strange and the remote, the
Romanticists of the late eighteenth and early seventeenth
centuries turned first of all to the Middle Ages for story
and for setting in an attempt to recreate the atmosphere
of the past.   In modern times any unknown place or
region will do as well as the Middle Ages.   The Realist,
on the other hand, endeavors to portray those conditions,
happenings, and people with which he is familiar in daily
life, and which most of us associate with the humdrum
and the commonplace.   Then, again, Romance revels in
the supernatural, the weird, the ghostly.   The Realist will
have nothing to do with anything so fantastical; he con-
fines himself to the facts that common sense accepts.
This Romantic love of strangeness predicates naturally
a fondness for adventure where curiosity and enthusiasm
may be satisfied in the excitement of stirring events.   But

---

* See Appendix V, "A Brief Summary of the Definitions of
Romanticism and Realism," and also Appendix VI, "Bibliography
on Romanticism and Realism."

the Realist is interested in the meaning of the everyday actions of ordinary people, in the representation of the usual incidents of contemporary life. If he should ever introduce shipwrecks, revolutions, murders, suicides, into his plots, or permit sailors, anarchists, savages, heroes, to enter his pages, it would be only in order that he might vivisect their symptoms and reactions according to the established impartial attitude of scientific investigation,— never that he might carry his readers away with the glamour of the adventure *per se,* as the Romancer loves to do.

In his search for individuality of experience the Romanticist turns to the lonely places of the earth, to Nature in its freest form. He seeks the elemental; the vast sweep of sky and ocean, the winds and the tempests, the mountains and the stars become to him the embodiment of the wonder of the world in which he finds himself imprisoned. This gives rise to that enthusiasm over Nature as setting which we associate with the Romantic school. On the contrary, the Realist is more interested in the study of environment; that is, of the social heredity of his characters, of the physical environment only in so far as it molds them, primarily of the social environment, including the industrial, educational, political, religious, and local surroundings. The opportunities which these conditions offer and their influence on the characters, and the latters' control over these circumstances, form the basis of the plot of the realistic novel.

Between the Romanticist and the Realist there exists a distinction more essential, however, than the mere selection of subject matter; that is, the individuality of the

method in which each treats the given material. In the
first place, the Romanticist creates through his imagination in broad outlines, suggestive rather than specific;
whereas the Realist must adopt the scientific method.   He
observes, analyzes, experiments, synthesizes proved facts
not hypotheses.   He uses reason rather than imagination.
He psychologizes rather than interprets.   The Realist
gives us the untouched negative; the Romanticist the
idealized picture.   To the Realist, as Zola says,

> "Imagination is no longer the predominating quality
> of the novelist. . . . Since imagination is no longer
> the ruling quality of the novelist, what, then, is to
> replace it?   There must always be a ruling quality.
> Today the ruling characteristic of the novelist is the
> sense of reality. . . . The sense of reality is to feel
> nature and to be able to picture her as she is.
> . . . In the same way that they formerly said of a
> novelist, 'He has imagination,' I demand that they
> should say today, 'He has a sense of reality.'   This
> will be grander and more just praise.   The ability to
> see is less common, even, than creative power."

The traditional view, therefore, is that the Romanticist
constructs through his imagination and an instinctive perception of the fitness of things; a Realist, through his
observation and his reason.

Now, in the second place, in order to create excitement
and wonder, the Romanticist builds up a plot full of suspense, surprise, and contrast, beginning with a definite
provocative incident and culminating in a thrilling
climax; such a plot as Ben Jonson defines in his discussion of the laws of the drama:

> "The fable is called the imitation of one entire and
> perfect action, whose parts are so joined and knit
> together, as nothing in the structure can be changed,
> or taken away, without impairing or troubling the

whole, of which there is a proportionable magnitude, in the numbers,"

a definition which he lifted bodily from Aristotle's *Poetics*.

But the Realist may go so far as not to have any plot at all in this usually accepted meaning of the word. De Maupassant says:

> "After the literary schools which have sought to give us a deformed, superhuman, poetic, tender, charming, or superb vision of life, there has come a realistic or naturalistic school, which professes to show us the truth, and nothing but ' the truth. . . . The incidents are disposed and graduated to the climax and the termination, which is the crowning decisive event, satisfying all the curiosity awakened at the beginning, barring any further interest, and terminating so completely the story told that we no longer desire to know what will happen to the personages who charmed our interest. . . . The novelist, on the other hand, who professes to give us an exact image of life ought carefully to avoid any concatenation of events that seem exceptional. His object is not to tell a story, to amuse us, to touch our pity, but to compel us to think, and to understand the deep, hidden meaning of events. Through having seen and meditated, he looks at the universe, things, facts, and men, in a manner peculiar to himself, the result of the combined effect of observation and reflection. He seeks to impart to us this personal vision of the world by reproducing it in his book. In order to move us as he himself has been moved by the spectacle of life, he must reproduce it before our eyes with scrupulous accuracy. He will have, then, to compose his work so skilfully, with such apparent simplicity, as to conceal his plot and render it impossible to discover his intentions . . . One can understand how such a manner of composition, so different from the old method, apparent to all eyes, often bewilders the critics, and that they do not discover the fine, secret, almost invisible threads employed by certain modern artists in place of the single thread which was called the 'plot'."

In regard to setting, also, there is a difference in treatment. Instead of the detailed and sometimes photographic description of surroundings and explanations of environmental conditions which the Realist assembles, we find in the works of the Romanticist a more pictorial description of place setting, and especially of Nature, in broader masses of color, of light, of shadow, of sound, aiming at the creation of an emotional tone and producing a subtle artistic effect. The Romanticist looks for beauty in all things. Sometimes his treatment of setting may be symbolic.

The broader method of the Romanticist appears again in his portrayal of the dramatis personæ of his stories. Instead of characters analyzed in careful detail which it is the chief aim of all Realists to create, we see in Romantic fiction vaguer outlines, characters less specialized and less complex,—types, in fact, rather than individuals.

Subject matter, method of treatment,—these are two essential differences between the Romanticist and the Realist. But these are not all. There exists a third factor which is the fundamental distinction, for out of it these first arise; that is, a divergency in the attitude of each towards life. This proceeds from the spirit of the man himself. Both are seekers for truth. But the Realist finds the truth in facing the facts of life as he can observe them with complete impartiality and disillusionment. He strives to attain an impersonal, objective point of view; he puts sympathy outside the pale. His purpose, in so far as he will avow a purpose, is altruistic because he believes that the exact revelation of life as it is, based on scientific evidence obtained from his own experience, is in itself moral; the universal as revealed through the specific is his aim, and knowledge rather than wisdom his goal. "We teach the bitter science of life, we give the high lesson of reality," says Zola.

The Romanticist cannot rest content with such practical didacticism. Life to him is not "a bitter science"; it is a glorious art. As Stevenson says,

> "The great creative writer shows us the realization and apotheosis of the day-dreams of common men. His stories may be nourished with the realities of life, but their true mark is to satisfy the nameless longings of the reader, and to obey the ideal laws of the day-dream. . . . Fiction is to the grown man what play is to the child; it is there that he changes the atmosphere and the tenor of his life; and when the game so chimes with his fancy that he can join in it with all his heart, when it pleases him with every turn, when he loves to recall it and dwells upon its recollection with entire delight, fiction is called romance."

To the writer of romance, then, illusion is his life-breath, and wonder the blood in his veins. He stands "silent, upon a peak in Darien," looking out over the magnificent spectacle of life, quivering with beauty, with passion, with ardor, life half revealed, half concealed in a flood of the light of mystery. He is eager to explore the mystery; he pushes on toward the illimitable horizon of life, baffled now by the inscrutability of fate, now by the pathos of human suffering, at times quieted by the serenity of experience past; but eternally young in soul, urged on by a "divine discontent," he aspires to his vision of the spiritual.

It has been frequently taken for granted that no man can be both Romanticist and Realist, because, as Clayton

Hamilton puts it, "the distinction is not external but internal; it dwells in the mind of the novelist; it is a matter for philosophic, not literary investigation." Brander Matthews says of the novelist: "Either he delights in the Classic or else he prefers the Romantic; for him to be an electic is a stark impossibility."

But is this absolute? May it not be possible for a writer to treat the subject matter of Romance in the method of a realist? May not a genius so combine method and matter with the imagination of a great scientist and the technique of a great artist,—in other words, with the keen perception and broad vision of the seer,—as to create neither Romance nor Reality, but Actuality itself?

"Perhaps," says a modern writer apropos of ethics, quoted by Neilsen in his *Essentials of Poetry,* "all theories of practice tend, as they rise to their best, as understood by their worthiest representatives, to identification with each other." And Mr. Neilsen goes on to say, "The supreme artists at their best rise above conflicts and propaganda, and are known, not by the intensity of their partisanship, but by the perfection of their balance. They show the virtues of all the schools; and in them each virtue is not weakened, but supported, by the presence of others which lesser men had supposed to be antagonistic." It is the man who sees in the romantic situations in which the most humdrum daily life abounds the realities of all human experience, who can transcribe them now with the impersonal observation of the scientist, now with the vision of the poet, who best reproduces for us the actuality of human life.

The Romantic-Realist, then, aims to translate into the medium of fiction life as it actually is. Both the·real and the romantic are inherent in all human affairs; and Realism or Romanticism is, after all, a matter of emphasis.

The Romanticist will look for those conditions or appearances of life which will create for men pure entertainment and relaxation by lifting them out of the commonplace and the complex. Man, when he wants to lose himself, demands above all else that "something be doing." A Romanticist, therefore, is interested primarily in happenings; he seeks for "some act or attitude that shall be remarkably striking to the mind's eye," as Stevenson puts it. The most irresistible appeal of romance, Walter Raleigh says, is not to the eye nor to the reason, but to the blood, "to all that dim instinct of danger, mystery and sympathy in things that is man's oldest inheritance—to the superstitions of the heart." The Romanticist finds out the unusual, the heroic, the imaginatively stimulating in the occurrences of daily life, and lays emphasis upon them. He sweeps us on by sheer intensity of action through a series of events with alternate checks of mystery, terror, premonition, suspense, to surprise and climax. In this zest for doing we do not pause to weigh the subtleties of motive nor to analyze the niceties of psychological distinctions in character evolution. We know the men and women of the story by their deeds. As to whether they be unalterably scientific products of their environment or not, the Romancer does not examine too profoundly. Certain eras, certain physical surroundings, they must belong to in order to make

possible the things they do, whether the romance be
historical, piratical, or Londonesque. This background
may be merely suggested or may be elaborately depicted
with all the photographic detail of the most dyed-in-the-
wool Realist. Stevenson, for example, is minutely
accurate in the description of latitude, longitude, winds,
and islands in the account of the voyage of the Farallone,
or again in the enumeration of the motley accumulation
of ship lumber piled in Attwater's dusty storehouse, or
the careful marshalling of details that is a running
commentary to the whole plot of *The Wrecker*,—that
grown-up *Treasure Island*.

But this realistic detail, although it plays upon our
credulity that the extraordinary tale be real, is, after all,
incidental, and hardly holds our attention so eager are
we to press on to the real business,—the progress of
events. To the Romanticist the world serves only as
the *mise en scène* for things that happen. At times this
background is merely pictorial, at times it is fatefully
symbolic; but it possesses always the glamour of the
unusual or a delightful suggestiveness discovered in the
usual. Into the deeds of men and this picture that frames
them, the Romanticist reads the mystery of all human
existence. The great Romanticist is gifted with the
language of a poet to suggest that mystery, and to unveil
what he has found of its meaning.

It may be that a novelist will choose to lay his emphasis
only on aspects such as these,—that which we call
Romance. It may be that he will choose to combine or
to vary this emphasis with another that more properly
belongs to the school of Realism. He may, to be sure,

relate the surprising, even the bizarre that faces the world
in all parts of the globe,—common places and remote
regions;—but he may relate those happenings not as
adventures for the sake of entertainment pure and simple,
but as dramas of gradually unfolding motive and character.   He will search out the puzzle of individuality, that
which makes the study of every life more intriguing than
the unraveling of the most involved detective story.   He
may examine into the effects of environment on a man's
character or his destiny without losing any of the artist's
appreciation of the beauty or the horror of the environment as background.   Ordinary seeming men and women
evolve in his hands from the simple, firm outlines to
which a career of events alone moulds them into subtly
modeled individuals.   He may keep the impersonal, un-
emotional attitude of the realist, that belongs to the scientific investigator, together with the perception of the
nobility of life and of the spiritual significance of man
that belongs to the philosopher and the poet.   And, above
all, he may possess that transcendent quality of style
which at once reveals and veils the beauty, the glory, the
fatality, the mystery of actuality as we know and live it.
This is to be a Romantic-Realist.   Of such rare union of
scientist, seer, and poet is the genius of Joseph Conrad.

We have seen that Romantic-Realism arises primarily
from a perception of the actual.   Now actuality must be
realized through experience; that is, through action and
observation reassembled and emphasized in the memory,
directed and harmonized through the reason, and interpreted through the imagination.   Given judgment and
imagination and observation, therefore, it follows that the

richer the experience and the sharper the memory, the deeper will be the perception of actuality. Fate took a hand, it would seem, in schooling Joseph Conrad in these very qualities. A Polish boy of aristocratic family, trained in home and in university in the best traditions of the world's literature, he took service as a lad before the mast on a sailing vessel at Marseilles in 1874; and after four years of life on the Mediterranean, finally set foot in his longed-for goal, England. There at the age of twenty-one he learned that language in which he has since been proclaimed the most distinguished artist of the twentieth century. For twenty years longer he sailed all the seas of the world as common seaman, mate, and finally Master, in the English Merchant Service. Then, after these twenty-five years of toilsome and adventurous sailor's life, he left the sea and wrote his first novel, *Almayer's Folly*, published in 1895. Since then he has devoted himself wholly to writing.

That not even the slightest detail of all the crowded impressions of those twenty-five years at sea escaped Conrad's observation, his novels are standing proof. He has an astonishing memory not only for what he himself has passed through, but for the experiences of others of which he has heard. His unique autobiography, *A Personal Record*, reveals these two gifts on every page. Witness the accurate detail and imaginative re-creation of his account of how his granduncle ate a dog, a tale told him, long before, when he was a little boy; of that day in his walking trip through the Alps which proved to be the turning point in his life; of his first sight of the British flag on a ship in the harbor of Marseilles.

It is only the person of limited experience who denies the presence in everyday life of romantic situations and sensational incidents. A writer who aims at the presentation of all life, therefore, is justified in including much that in its bald statement may be called sensational, even lurid. Romance, sometimes melodrama, is the matter of every moment of existence. A citizen of a conservative Eastern city has only to read any San Francisco newspaper to be convinced of this. For instance, one afternoon, with pencil in hand, I glanced casually through a newspaper which had already that morning been read for world news. Call it the *Daily Occidental:* you remember what Stevenson says of it—"This was a paper (I know not if it be so still) that stood out alone among its brethren in the West; the others, down to their smallest item, were defaced with capitals, head lines, allitrations, swaggering misquotations, and the shoddy picturesque and unpathetic pathos of the Harry Millers: the *Occidental* alone appeared to be written by a dull, sane, Christian gentleman, singly desirous of communicating knowledge." Without either minute or industrious search I jotted down the following items. The mere enumeration of them reads like the headlines of movie shockers! I omit the daily long list of births and deaths, engagements, elopements, marriages, and the usual Western array of divorces. There were tales of heroism of soldiers and of nurses in the daily business of war. There were articles about an insane woman, an embezzlement, a suicide, a murder, a trial for poisoning. There was a story of the arrest of a released prisoner for petty theft one minute after he had finished serving his former

sentence, side by side with the account of a woman who
gave her blood in transfusion to save the life of an in-
jured man. I read of the explosion of bombs at a railway
station, of anarchy in Russia, of civil war in Costa Rica.
I was fascinated by the story of a quest for "untold
wealth." Read a paragraph or two of the unembellished
newspaper narrative of this last event:

> "Men have heeded the call of lost sapphires, and
> within the week the little eighty-ton schooner
> "Casco," that carried Robert Louis Stevenson to the
> islands of romance, will poke her nose through the
> Golden Gate and head for the frozen northland . . .
> "Many centuries ago when China was young, there
> was a great war. The most powerful king led his
> armies to battle and vanquished the other armies.
> Then he died.
> "The king had been noted for his fondness of
> sapphires. His subjects, worshipping his memory,
> made annual pilgrimages to his tomb, and each de-
> posited at the burial place one or two sapphires.
> That insured the pilgrim's speedy entry into the
> happy hereafter.
> "Centuries passed, as is their wont. A natural
> disaster swept away the tomb, and nothing remained
> except the legend. Then the glacier that had covered
> the tomb wore away, and an adventurer that traveled
> the North found the treasure.
> "The man carried away all the sapphires he could
> carry. He planned to return for the rest, but he died
> too soon.
> "The men of the "Casco" have a map, they say,
> that directs them to a spot beyond the beyond, far
> north in Northern Siberia, where lie heaps and heaps
> of sapphires that the worshippers laid at the tomb
> of the 'Great One'."

How will those thirty men come out of that adventure?
How will those thirty lonely souls react upon each other?
What a Conrad tale lies hidden there!

Well, here you have in one morning's paper, heaped

promiscuously together, love, joy, tragedy, suffering, self-sacrifice, heroism and depravity, insanity and crime, revolution and anarchy, adventure and buried treasure. This is the material out of which Joseph Conrad has built his stories: a search for buried gold, the explosion of a bomb, the plotting of anarchists and spies, a revolution in Costa Rica and another in Spain, shipwrecks and pirates, cannibalism and savagery, murder, love, beauty, fate, self-seeking, and heroism.

Yet such events as these, which lie at the heart of all Romance, become in the hands of Conrad not in the least mere exciting adventures in the circumstantial objective sense, but adventures far more tense and intricate, adventures of the spirit. Every story which he has written is a psychological study of the soul of a man or a woman. Better than any other writer, Conrad has succeeded in conveying to us the sense of the profound mystery that wraps every human being, that perception we all have of "man's incapacity for self-realization," that puzzled sympathy with man's suffering, that recognition of the irony of fate, of the inscrutability of nature, of the eternal mutability of all things; and finally our baffled realization that at the end, even, nothing is clear. Such is life in actuality, and such is life in Conrad's tales.

With the poetic imagination of the Romanticist and the minute observation of the Realist, Conrad assembles into an impersonal study of motives, conduct, and character that is at once as restrained and as passionate as life itself, those incongruous and startling incidents, or those apparently matter-of-fact occurrences which side by side throng past us in daily existence. On the significance

of these happenings Conrad fixes our attention, always
with the high purpose of presenting life as it actually is.

In the famous artistic creed, written in 1905, and now
published as the Preface to *The Nigger of the Narcissus,*
Conrad has unflinchingly and clearly proclaimed his belief
in this fundamental verity of all true art in fiction.   The
very conjunction of words in the title to this book by
which, he says, he is willing to stand or fall, is emblematic
of Conrad's vision of life.   He says in part:

> "A work that aspires, however humbly, to the con-
> dition of art should carry its justification in every
> line.   And art itself may be defined as a single-
> minded attempt to render the highest kind of justice
> to the visible universe, by bringing to light the truth,
> manifold and one, underlying its every aspect.
> . . . The artist, then, like the thinker or the scientist,
> seeks the truth and makes his appeal.   . . . But the
> artist appeals to that part of our being which is a gift
> and not an acquisition—and, therefore, more perma-
> nently enduring.   He speaks to our capacity for
> delight and wonder, to the sense of mystery sur-
> rounding our lives: to our sense of pity and beauty
> and pain: to the latent feeling of fellowship with all
> creation—and to the subtle but invincible conviction
> of solidarity that knits together the loneliness of
> innumerable hearts to the solidarity in dreams, in
> joy, in sorrow, in aspirations, in illusions, in hope, in
> fear, which binds men to each other, which binds all
> humanity—the dead to the living and the living to the
> unborn.   . . . To snatch in a moment of courage, from
> the remorseless rush of time, a passing phase of life
> is only the beginning of the task.   The task ap-
> proached in tenderness and faith is to hold up
> unquestioningly, without choice and without fear, the
> rescued fragment before all eyes in the light of a
> sincere mood.   It is to show its vibration, its color,
> its form; and through its movement, its form and its
> color, reveal the substance of its truth—disclose its
> inspiring secret: the stress and passion within the
> core of each convincing moment.   In a single-minded
> attempt of that kind, if one be deserving and fortun-

ate, one may perchance attain to such clearness of sincerity that at last the presented vision of regret or pity, of terror or mirth, shall awaken in the hearts of the beholders that feeling of unavoidable solidarity; of the solidarity in mysterious origin, in toil, in joy, in hope, in uncertain fate, which binds men to each other and all mankind to the visible world."

This is the Summum Bonum of literary endeavor. It cannot be confined within the narrow limits of Realism nor of Romance. There is no term which fully comprehends its whole import. If it were permissible, we might attempt to coin a word, *Aletheism* (Greek, 'Αλήθεια, *truth*) the truth of life; that would best express it. But even the most philological of invented words is awkward; and instead we must substitute the circumlocution *Romantic-Realism*.

In what ways, then, has Conrad fulfilled his own creed?

PART II

The Romantic-Realism of Method in Plot and Character Development

ONE of the most individual of the many distinctive things about Conrad is his method of presenting his stories. It has irritated some critics, pleased others, puzzled them all. Many times objected to, it has been more often defended, especially by the later writers about Conrad who have come to see that the intricacy of his method is the expression of the man himself. Henry James has said that it seems to him that Conrad has deliberately set himself the problem of doing a thing in the hardest way possible for pure pleasure in the difficulty of the task. Certain it is that a Conrad story seldom presents itself as a straightforward narrative in the old comfortable chronological sequence of cause and effect, ditto, ditto, to the climax of events, which, the formulas propone, should be usually,—in stories of adventure or mystery, always,—as surprising as possible, and decorously saved until the very end of the tale. In other words, we have grown used to the cut-and-dried plot of incident that fulfills all expectations and leaves characters and situations settled forever afterwards.

But Conrad does not often construct his stories in this conventional way. He has been accused of having no plot

30

at all in some of his tales; and in the accepted romantic use of the term, this is true. De Maupassant's explanation of plot in the realistic novel has been quoted above. Undoubtedly this method of the Realists has been used by Conrad at times. True to his own artistic creed, he does not confine himself to any one literary form. He has shown us in *Typhoon, The Secret Sharer,* or *The Shadow Line,* for instance, that he can when he wishes construct a stereotyped plot of incident. Yet his more frequent method is to depict a few months or years of "a life for the purpose of showing its peculiar and characteristic significance in relation to all the beings that surround it," or even in relation to the development of its own soul. It is *The Nigger of the Narcissus* that most obviously reveals this purpose of structure. Little really happens: a ship starts to sea with a crew usual enough but for one puzzling exception; a storm comes up; the officers quell an incipient mutiny; a man dies of lingering disease, and is buried at sea; the ship reaches port, and the crew disperses—that is all. Yet how unforgettable a story it is! Here is a powerful study two hundred pages long of the meaning of one phase of the "spectacle of life" as reflected in the reactions of a small group of men. Like life, it is inclusive; like life, it is profoundly significant.

This tale is the most extreme instance of the absence of apparent plot evolution, for Conrad is too much of a Romanticist to give himself over wholly to the manner of the Realists. He loves incident, exciting, bizarre, commonplace; and something definitely happens in all of his stories. But these incidents are not of interest for the sake of the event alone. They shape a life or form a character. Yet this, as in actuality, we comprehend some time afterwards. And that is the key to the seemingly topsy-turvy method of Conrad's plot construction. It is only *after* things have happened that we realize what it all meant; or we see the result, and begin to piece together bit by bit the series of happenings that have brought it to pass. Out of our memory, from conversations or hints of others, from fragments narrated now and then in a mood of reminiscence by the actors themselves, we build up the story of what has gone before to make what now is. Flashes of insight help us, reasoned analyses must fill in the gaps; and too often much remains that will always be inexplicable. If this is life—and who will deny it—should it not also be art? Why have the audacity to demand of a novelist omniscience? Conrad's is the rare genius of putting before us through the medium of language the actuality of life itself. We have come to demand that fiction spread out before us a topographical map of the lives of the characters with every path and cross-road and chasm neatly labelled to our complete satisfaction. It annoys some readers to be asked to use their own imagination and their own wits. They do not realize the tremendous compliment paid them by this writer who presupposes that his readers have his own power of intuition to foresee events already hinted at, to study personalities, to deduce philosophies, and with retrospective wisdom to fit together what at the time appeared an illogical jumble.

Almost every one of Conrad's stories, therefore, progresses retrogressively. We start out with a personality

in a certain situation, as in *Lord Jim*, for example, and
gradually we learn how he came to be where he is; or
we stop in the middle of an episode to pick up the threads
of past events that will account for the state of mind
or the actions which are to follow, as in *Under Western
Eyes* or *Nostromo* or *Victory*; or we face an unaccountable condition of affairs and are forced to go back to
trace out little by little how it came to be, as in *The
Nigger of the Narcissus* or *Heart of Darkness*.

A man's previous history may be only implied until
late in the book when it becomes necessary to reveal the
whole story in order to explain the effect of his personality on others, and lead us to see how he alone could
be the agent in succeeding events. Dr. Monygham's
story, for example, is not told until nearly three hundred
and fifty pages of the novel in which he is one of the
important characters have been read. Often, it is to be
admitted, these sudden pauses in the rapid development
of events is irritating. We are out of patience with the
long exposition of Sotillo's maneuvers in the middle of
the most tense situation in *Nostromo.* Sometimes these
interruptions appear wholly irrelevant, as when we stop
to listen to the past history of the Chief Inspector or
read a description of the most minor characters who do
nothing in the story but form the partners in an insignificant game of cards, or read a picture of the previous
Police Commissioners of London in *The Secret Agent*.
It is difficult to restrain our impatience when Marlow
digresses from the story of Lord Jim to give us the biog-
raphies of such unimportant personages as little Bob
Stanton or Chester and Captain Robinson, picturesque

as they are. Mr. Conrad's enthusiasm over the details
of conversation as well as over the actuality of the background figures, leads him into over-emphasis on what
amounts to a quite banal conversation between Therese
and Monsieur George in one of his latest books,
The Arrow of Gold. We even have to stop to learn why
it is that Therese does not recognize a brougham when
she sees one. Such minute detail, realistic though it be,
has degenerated into a mannerism.

Since Conrad's object is to make the story known as
it would be in actuality, it is necessary that the events be
retold after they have happened. In order to do this,
Conrad uses a mouthpiece. The most famous is, of
course, Marlow. As to whether Marlow is to be identi-
fied with Conrad himself, much has been written. Marlow, whether he be Conrad in person or not, is symbolic.
We know real facts about him: that he is a retired sea
captain of middle age, for he joined the service when he
was "just twenty," and "it was twenty-two years ago,"
that he has "sunken cheeks, a yellow complexion, a
straight back, an ascetic aspect," that his experiences
have made him somewhat cynical, vastly conscious of the
irony of life, but unabatingly interested in all human
beings. He tells their stories in his own desultory, involved, and unending way, impersonally aloof "in the pose
of a meditating Buddha." He has an immitigable curiosity, and we hear again when he is in a reminiscent
mood the discoveries of that curiosity. In the new preface to *Lord Jim* which first appeared in an article in
The Bookman, Conrad answers the objection that no
one could believe that one man could talk for interminable

hours like Marlow and hold his audience. "After think-
ing it over for something like sixteen years I am not so
sure about that," he writes.   "Men have been known both
in the tropics and in the temperate zone, to sit up half
the night 'swapping yarns' . . . As to the mere physical
possibility we all know that some speeches in Parliament
have taken nearer six hours than three in delivery;
whereas all that part of the book which is Marlow's
narrative can be read through aloud, I should say, in less
than three hours."

Marlow holds his readers as he holds his hearers.
Through his mind we come to understand Lord Jim,
Flora de Barral, the officers of the "Judea."   The young
mate who tells the tale of Falk or the young captain of
The Secret Sharer might well be Marlow.   We cannot
help but feel that Mills, the inscrutable, "with his pene-
tration" in *The Arrow of Gold* is only Marlow under a
new name and in a different body.   But Mills, "the burly,
the rustic," is not so convincing as the lean and worn
Marlow, nor does he tell us the tale as he saw it happen.

Sometimes Marlow relates the story as a firsthand experience of his own, sometimes as others have told it to
him, even, as in *Chance*, as others have learned it from
others who have told it to him; so that we get that most
subtle play of mind on mind, the uttermost refinement of
the narrative point of view, like the cross lights of a
multiple reflector.   Many of the stories are told in the
impersonal third person of the author, as are *Nostromo*
and *The Secret Agent* and most of the short stories; some
in the first person, when they are confessedly reminiscences of Conrad himself, as *Almayer's Folly*, and, we

feel sure, *The Shadow Line;* or in the first person by
one of the dramatis personæ, as *The Arrow of Gold.* In
Under Western Eyes the point of view is more labored.
The story is told in the first person by the English teacher
of languages, partly as firsthand experiences of his own,
partly as direct transcribing of Razumov's journal, partly
as resumé of portions of the journal.   But the effect is
not always convincing.   In any case, Conrad, as I have
said, is anxious to avoid the traditional novelist's omniscience.   Even in tales of the third person like
Nostromo, much of the narrative is told by Captain
Mitchell.   Conrad even goes so far as to resort to literary
devices.   In the same novel it is through Martin Decoud's
letters to his sister (one of them written under circumstances preposterous even to our indulgent credulity)
that we learn what has been happening.   The diary of
Razumov in *Under Western Eyes,* the pages of Kurtz'
manuscript in *Heart of Darkness,* the letters of Captain
MacWhirr, Solomon Rout, and Jukes in *Typhoon,* the
reminiscences of Monsieur George in *The Arrow of Gold,*
are other examples of this device.

.In this later novel Conrad has attempted to disarm the
critics by writing a straightforward story, but his innate
propensity to retrogressive narrative gets the better of
him even here.   The situation, the place, the time, and the
characters are carefully explained to the reader in a pre-
paratory "Note," and the subsequent events *in so far as
they are known* (observe the Conradian reservation), in a
second note at the end.   In spite of all this elaborate preliminary explanation, however, we progress in the story in
the customary elliptical manner.   We stop and mark time

while Blunt tells Doña Rita's past history, or while Rita herself recounts in fuller detail what we have already learned briefly of her childhood days,—the epoch in her life that furnishes the key to the whole story of her actions.

Sometimes the preliminary narrative is definitely symbolic as is the Prelude in *Nostromo*. Sometimes the conclusion is told us long before the whole thread of the plot has been unraveled. Twice in *Nostromo*, more than a hundred pages before the end, we are carried forward, and then go back to learn the events that completed the crisis in the story at which we had been halted. In *Under Western Eyes* the whole of the second and third parts happens *after* the larger portion of the fourth part. By the time we have reached Part IV we have, of course, surmised the facts we are to learn in it. Again in *The Rescue*, although the unfolding of the plot is for the most part simple and direct, Conrad has several times resorted to retroaction to interpret a present situation. At the end of the story the explanation of the stroke of fate by which Lingard, the indomitable, has been transformed into the crushed and dazed figure which arouses in us, as in young Carter, solicitude and compassion, involves a succession of steps backward through the preceding thirty-six hours.

This retrospective method of narration is startling until we realize that Conrad has been trusting to our intuition of the dénouement. In fact, we should be stupid indeed if we did not perceive the inevitable outcome of what has passed before our eyes, for we have had sign after sign laid before us. Here again Conrad departs from the strictness of realistic method to sound the romantic note of forewarning. Not a single one of his stories is

constructed without it. Time and time again we are told
of the "something ominous," or meet a "startled pause"
in the trend of events. It may be a premonition, as it is
sometimes in daily life, like Marlow's uneasiness on beginning his voyage to the heart of darkness; it may be
a prediction like that of Captain Giles about the dangers
of the Gulf of Siam to the young captain in *The Shadow
Line;* it may be an incident that should have served for
a portent as the narrator realizes too late, such as
Monsieur George's strange encounter with the comic
Mephistophelean Ortega; it may be mere superstition, as
when the rats left the "Judea" after it was supposed that
she was at last in ship-shape condition. In some stories
Conrad himself deliberately hints of events to come, as
often in *Nostromo.* Frequently the forewarnings are
symbolic. This is true of the descriptions of setting,
notably in *Almayer's Folly, Heart of Darkness, The
Secret Agent, Nostromo.* Even the title may be a symbol,
as in *The Arrow of Gold.* The characters themselves
may openly declare the symbolism, as do both Rita and
Monsieur George of the arrow, piercing yet golden, and
finally vanished forever. The name of Lingard's brig is
symbolic of the lightning flash of beauty and of passion
with the thunderbolts of fate that is woven in golden
threads throughout the setting in *The Rescue.*

When after nights of fruitless agony, Razumov wakes
to gaze on the lamp in his study and finds it burned out,
he calls it in bitter forecast, "the extinguished beacon
of his labors, a cold object of brass and porcelain, among
the scattered pages of his notes and small piles of books—
a mere litter of blackened paper—dead matter—without

significance or interest." With Russian mysticism, as he returns from his confession, dripping wet from the thunder-storm that has passed over him, he mutters in answer to the solicitude of his landlord, "Yes, I am washed clean." Many seemingly chance remarks of the characters prove to be symbolic premonitions of events. One of the most conscious of these is Señora's Teresa's curse on Nostromo when he refuses to go for a priest as she lies dying.

Sometimes these forecasts are ironical as well as symbolic. But usually it is not until the story is well advanced that we become aware of the pregnancy of these brief statements. A great part of the intensity of the crisis in *The Secret Agent* arises from the ironic prevision of what is to happen. "The excellent husband of Winnie Verloc saw no writing on the wall." And later, "Mr. Verloc wallowed on his back. But he longed for a more perfect rest—for sleep—for a few hours of delicious forgetfulness. That would come later." In how different a way from what he had meant was that fateful sentence fulfilled!

In some of the tales, and particularly in the later books, this dramatic forewarning, ironic or symbolic or both, becomes the motif of the story and occurs again and again like a varied refrain. In *Nostromo* the theme of the evil influence of the San Tomé silver mine that enslaved and deadened all, is sounded in the Prelude, and reëchoes throughout the long story until the book closes on the same note when we hear Linda's "true cry of love and grief that seemed to ring aloud from Punta Mala to Azuera and away to the bright line of the horizon, overhung by a big white cloud shining like a mass of solid silver.' In *Chance* the dominant note is struck in the title and sounds again and again throughout the story. In *The Arrow of Gold* we hear from the beginning to the end the theme of the symbolism of Rita in whom is "something of the women of all time," whose face "drew irresistibly one's gaze to itself by an indefinable quality of charm beyond all analysis and made you think of remote races, of strange generations, of the faces of women sculptured on immemorial monuments and of those lying unsung in their tombs." Rita herself says, "I am as old as the world."

Because of this use of an ever-recurrent theme and of many premonitions, Conrad may be thought definitely to renounce all attempt to surprise or mystify his readers. Yet there are episodes in all of his stories which puzzle us as much as the actors themselves, others which keep us in breathless suspense, others which confound us with their unexpectedness. Who can ever forget that tense situation in *Nostromo* when Decoud and the capataz de cargadores, crossing the gulf with the treasure, in the blackness of the night as if "launched into space," are projected suddenly into that startling adventure with Hirsh and Sotillo's fleet? The strain is almost as severe on us as on the composure of the actors themselves. *The Secret Sharer* is one tense question from beginning to end. Will he be discovered? We shudder at every narrow escape. The suspense and mystery of the first part of *The Secret Agent* is spoiled only for those who have been so unfortunate as to have read beforehand a book review that reveals the whole plot. In *The Arrow of Gold* we are as taken aback as Monsieur George to find when he turns around in what he supposed an empty room, "a woman's dress on a chair, other articles of apparel scattered about." The sudden explosion of the coal in the hold of the "Judea" when "everybody was on the broad grin" after their successful quenching of the fire, leaves our eyes like saucers, and our mouths open too. The unexpected climax of Big Brierley's history, in *Lord Jim*, is as astonishing as it was to those who knew him in real life. We are as horror-struck as the young captain in *The Shadow Line* to make the fateful discovery that there is no quinine on his fever-ridden ship.

Often this suspense in which we have been held tense and the sudden crash of the unexpected are accompanied by a terror that is Homeric in its minuteness of horrible detail. Impressed upon our memory by the very horror of it is the scene of finding Hirsh's body in *Nostromo*, or the uncanny burial of James Wait in *The Nigger of the Narcissus*, or the gruesome description of the mangled remains of Steevie in *The Secret Agent*.

Sometimes the mystery of the plot is solved for us, as in *The Secret Agent* or *Falk*. More often it is a mystery of character which is left forever baffling. The solution lies in our own ability to read between the lines of what is told us. Such is the mystery of *The Arrow of Gold;* such, too, is the mystery of *The Heart of Darkness*. It is interesting to contrast with the latter a story called *Out There* by Grant Watson in which everything that Conrad only implies is elaborately made clear; the contrast serves to show the power of Conrad's method of repression.

This same repression appears also as condensation of narrative; and in this respect Conrad's tales are unlike the romantic stories of adventure in which each new deed of the hero is detailed at full length. How many chapters might Scott or even Stevenson have made of this one brief sentence that falls in the heart of the novel!

> "One evening I found myself weary, heartsore, my brain still dazed and with awe in my heart entering Marseilles by way of the railway station, after many adventures, one more disagreeable than another, involving privations, great exertions, a lot of difficulties with all sorts of people who looked upon me evidently more as a discreditable vagabond deserving the attention of gendarmes than a respectable (if crazy) young gentleman attended by a guardian angel of his own."

We never hear any more of this part of his adventures; it has no bearing on the main theme. Anyway, it had all been told before in the story of "The Tremolino" in *The Mirror of the Sea*.

This restraint in selection is governed by the theme of the story and by the dominant traits of the characters. To Conrad these two become one. The motivation of the characters is the theme of the story. Nothing arises in the course of events which is not the outcome of character; for in Conrad, in the same sense as is true in Shakespeare, character is destiny, plus that inexplicable something, call it accident or pure fate, that the great creative writers of all time have seen unfolding before their eyes in human life. Each of Conrad's tales becomes, then, an adventure of a soul, that new kind of adventure which Ernest Rhys speaks of in his essay on *Romance*: "It may even be said that today we have widened the avenues of imagination, instead of closing them, as many people suppose; for we have learned to find in new areas, and in the more intimate regions of psychology, spiritual adventures which are more real than anything told in the romances of chivalry." Almost inevitably the outcome of the adventure is tragedy, for Conrad sees as the irony of life that the predominating quality of a man's character is invariably the one that fate chooses to try. At times man is triumphant, at times the victor is fate. Nostromo's colossal belief in his own incorruptibility and his eager desire to uphold his reputation for absolute trustworthiness prove in the end the means to his undoing. Lord Jim eating his heart out with a sense of his lost honor, Kurtz avid of power, Heyst determined to be the skeptical onlooker, Razumov unfaithful to the supreme confidence imposed in him, Captain MacWhirr unacquainted with imaginative fear, are all of them drawn into the mesh of circumstance that chance weaves around them to put to the proof that particular quality. Conrad's men and women are "haunted by a fixed idea," to use his own phrase. It is Conrad's object to discover "a complete singleness of motive behind the varied manifestations of a consistent character." Every link in the series of happenings is chosen to fix our attention upon the temperamental uniqueness that constitutes the individual.

Every story thus becomes the history of one being around which are grouped the other personages of the plot, to further or obstruct the life of the protagonist. *Lord Jim, Almayer's Folly, The End of the Tether, Falk, Youth, Heart of Darkness,* center around one figure whose personality is the focus of the whole story. Be-

cause of the intimacy of human relationships, most of the
novels draw close within the circle of the life of the
chief character that one other human being as markedly
individual as himself.   These are the women whose personality involves the fate of the men.   Winnie Verloc,
Lena, Natalie Haldin, Nina, Doña Rita, Edith Travers,
are inseparable from the articulated pattern of the plot.
In such masterpieces as *The Nigger of the Narcissus* and
Nostromo this narrowed character focus has expanded
to include the whole character groups, so vital and so
real that the book takes on epic proportions.   We are
moving in a world of human beings as various and as
crowded as the real universe.   We are as convinced of
their actuality as we are of that of the people we know.

All of Conrad's characters have in them that univer-
sality which we call type; but it is the type arising from
established careers or environments rather than from
personality itself.   The largest class of these types is
men of the sea: sailors, mates, captains; adventurers and
derelicts.   Men of the land, too, are there: anarchists,
plotters of revolutions and of bomb outrages; occasionally
financiers, men of the world of society.   And among
them we meet the women, fewer in number, all with a
certain mysterious quality in their taciturnity, whether
they be savage or cockney, women respectably bourgeoise
or picaresque.   But it is in the minor characters only
that we find pure type in Conrad; and that is in those who
are needed to fill in the background, like the South
Americans in *Nostromo* or the Chinamen in *Typhoon*, or
the lesser revolutionists in *Under Western Eyes*.   Several
photographic portraits of individuals in the crowd serve

to suggest the *milieu* in which the story is to move; but for the most part these minor personages are a background mass which our imaginations are to conjure up from the selected types given us. It is not for type that Conrad is seeking, but for the individual. It is in the indiviuality of personality that his interest lies. To search out the intimate motives and the inexpressible secrets of each man or woman who moves through those circumstances in which it has pleased life to place them is the problem of his tales; only in this respect can Conrad be called a writer of problem novels. He never preaches. He puts before us as some one else has seen it the actions of another human being, and lets us create with him the thoughts, the motives, the resolves which led to those actions.

For this reason, too, then, he needs an interpreter. It is only by glimpses that we comprehend other people. This is true even of those whom we know best and flatter ourselves that we understand most thoroughly,—those whom we say we can read like a book. How much more is this true of those whom we know only casually! Visual impressions, disconnected incidents at occasional meetings only, reported conversations, supposed motives, must be put together to form our estimate of the man himself. Our own imagination and reason must fit the fragments, large or small, symmetrical or irregular, into the mosaic of the whole until the completed design stand revealed. There are bound to be some blank spaces in the end, some still remaining mystery that blurs the colors and the clear outlines.

The history of others can be reflected only through the

medium of another personality. To create the veri-
similitude of this medium is Conrad's object. Therefore
we find almost always when we are introduced to each
important character the indirect method of exposition
proceeding by degrees to the direct. We hear of So-and-
So first in a casual way: that it is Mrs. Gould, the only
English woman in Sulaco, who has given old Giorgio
Viola his Bible in Italian; or that it is Captain Mitchell's
capataz de cargadores to whom all the Europeans in
Sulaco owe their preservation in the recent revolution,—
"Nostromo, a man absolutely above reproach," the mere
sight of whose black whiskers and white teeth was enough
to quell all the town leperos. Marlow tells the author
that there was only one of Mrs. Fyne's girl-friends whom
he had conversed with at all, and proceeds to narrate their
accidental and unusual meeting. "Her arched eyebrows
frowned above her blanched face. . . . She looked
unhappy." Slowly we comprehend that this rude and
bitter girl is the heroine around the riddle of whose personality is to revolve this strange tale of *Chance*. Mills,
who has seen Doña Rita only twice, can already say of
her: "I am not an easy enthusiast where women are con-
cerned, but she was without doubt the most admirable
find of his amongst all the priceless items he had accumu-
lated in that house—the most admirable."

When we are at length introduced to the character to
talk with him or to observe him in person, we receive,
first of all, a general impression of physical appearance,
it may be only of the most notable traits of dress or of
feature. Mrs. Gould is the only lady present at the
ceremony of the turning of the first sod for the National

Central Railway of Costaguana, and we know her at once as we read, "Mrs. Gould's appearance was made youthful by the mobile intelligence of her face." Gradually we learn to know that she is a little lady with a low laugh and gray eyes, "her little face attractively overweighted by great coils of hair, whose mere parting seemed to breathe upon you the fragrance of frankness and generosity." But before this we have come to perceive her vivacity, her charm, and her sympathetic influence on all who know her. It is not until he has been taking an active part in the story that has progressed nearly a hundred and fifty pages that we see what Nostromo really looks like. True to this point of view, Razumov's appearance is not described to us until the narrator of the story, the language teacher, meets him in person when the tale is already half told.

Sometimes, on the contrary, the method is frankly direct. *Almayer's Folly* and *Lord Jim*, for example, open with a picture of the hero and an explanation of what he is doing; then the narrative goes back immediately to a brief summary of his past life, and there begins the long story of what has led him to where he now is. The beginnings of *Il Conde* and of *Typhoon* are excellent examples of this method of Conrad's. In these stories we observe first the hero's appearance, and then we learn briefly his biography up to the day when the story begins. The stage directions are completed; the action can begin.

Conrad uses both methods, then: he begins at once with a fairly full description of the character, followed by a bit of biography and an explanation of his psy-

chology; or he leads us slowly to an acquaintance with
the body and soul of the man himself. In the earliest
novels he more frequently employs the first method with
special stress on the most striking qualities, emphasized
in the rest of the story by constant reiteration, and revealed by every incident in the series of events. In his
later books, however, he is more inclined to use the cumu-
lative method, sometimes, in fact, carrying it almost to
an extreme, as in *The Arrow of Gold,* in which the
portrait of Rita is pieced together item by item until we
are well into the story before we are sure of what she
really is like,—if we are ever wholly sure!

As the story progresses, the impression that the character makes tends to be simplified into one marked trait.
It may be the same that first acquaintance gave us; it
may have shifted to another emphasis. The character
has come to have for all with whom it is associated—
the other characters, narrator and reader—one significance. In order to crystallize this impression, Conrad
resorts to the Homeric emphasis of descriptive epithet.
These are woven in and out through the narrative like
recurrent patterns in a design. We learn to love Mrs.
Gould's "little head and shining coils of hair"; the beautiful Antonia appears always as "a tall grave girl" with
"full red lips"; Charles Gould in his "imperturbable
calm" is "the impenetrability of the embodied Gould
Concession." Nostromo appears in everyone's eyes, including his own, as "a man for whom the value of life
seems to consist in personal prestige." In *The Nigger
of the Narcissus* Donkin's "bat-like ears," his "shifty
eyes, and yellow hatchet-face" are emblematic of his in-

fluence among the crew. The derelict shade of Jörgensen is the tragic anticipation of what destiny has in store for Lingard. It is the bitter irony of Razumov's fate "to inspire confidence" in every one with whom he comes into contact, most tragically of all in "clear-eyed" Natalie Haldin. Winnie Verloc's "philosophy consisted in not taking notice of the inside facts"; she "felt profoundly that things do not stand much looking into"; she was "confirmed in her instinctive conviction that things don't bear looking into much"; she was aware that "it did not stand looking into much." In fact, in some of the later books, these epithetical phrases degenerate into mere catchwords. Winnie later in the novel becomes ironically "the widow of Mr. Verloc." Ossipon is "the robust Ossipon"; Verloc is "the heavy-lidded." In *The Arrow of Gold* Blunt is tagged in three phrases, two of them of his own invention: he is "the fatal Mr. Blunt," "*Américain, Catholique et gentilhomme*," "who lived by his sword." Rita in the same novel is the tawny-haired, the sapphire-eyed, for "the tawny halo of her unruly hair" and her "darkly-brilliant blue glance" shine resplendent through all the pages of Monsieur George's reminiscences.

In the portraits of minor characters this exaggeration of the significant attribute stands out as a caricature of the man,—unforgettable, decisive and comic. Such is the steward in *The Shadow Line* "with his face of an unhappy goat"; the comic-opera General Montero in *Nostromo*, the abominable and fatuous Ortega. In *Under Western Eyes* the artificiality of the famous Madame de S— is emphasized by her ghastly painted mask of a face, her gleaming false teeth, and fantastically

shining black eyes.   No less grotesque in appearance is
her scared, sallow-faced companion and even the huge
Peter Ivanovitch himself.   In *The Secret Agent* the un-
wieldy bulk of Michaelis is emphasized in every phrase,
as when he "uncrossed his thick legs, similar to bolsters."

It is indeed in descriptions of fat men that Conrad
derives a sardonic amusement from this over-emphasis of
the grotesque.   There is this same Michaelis, "round like
a tub"; Mr. Verloc, "undemonstrative and burly in a
fat-pig style," with podgy hands and a gross neck; and
Sir Ethelred, "expanded, enormous and weighty,"—three
exaggeratedly fat men in one book!   More unforgettable
is the obese captain of the *Patna,* like "'a trained baby
elephant walking on hind legs," and the manager of the
Eldorado Exploring Expedition in *Heart of Darkness*
who "carried his fat paunch with ostentation on his short
legs," and the terrible revolutionist Nikita surnamed
Necator whose squeaky voice and balloon-like stomach
are in burlesque contrast to his sinister deeds of violence.

But it is only the unpleasant characters whom Conrad
lashes with these cutting realistic phrases.   His portraits
can be as attractive as the persons themselves.   There is
Lord Jim "clean-limbed, clear-faced, firm on his feet, as
promising a boy as the sun ever shone on," the type of
fine, dependable, honest, and courageous youngster, whose
appearance so mysteriously and terribly belied what he
stood accused of.   There is Powell in *Chance.*   "The
red tint of his clear-cut face with trim short black
whiskers under a cap of curly iron-gray hair was the only
warm spot in the dinginess of that room cooled by the
cheerless tablecloth."

But a man who has lived long enough to have acquired
that complexity of experience which shapes him as an
individual worth the investigation of this novelist, is
seldom in point of fact a being to be described in terms
of the beautiful. He may be picturesque, he may be
attractive in his virility, he will probably be interesting,
but he does not usually impress one æsthetically. A
young man may be handsome and good to look upon like
Lord Jim; but in youth that is generally to be taken for
granted. Grown men are too marked by time and endurance to present that color, serenity, and grace of human
contour and feature that are the essence of beauty.
Hence it is that in the descriptions of men Conrad uses
the uncompromising method of the Realist; and reserves
the suggestiveness and poetry of the Romantic style for
descriptions of nature and of women. He turns for
beauty to women in the bloom of youth or of love. How
many of them there are, after all! Emilia Gould,
Antonia Avellanos, Linda Viola, and her sister Giselle,
Flora de Barral, Natalie Haldin, that magnificent young
girl, the niece of Hermann in *Falk*, even fair-haired Edith
Travers, the "representative woman," Nina, Almayer's
half-breed daughter, and last and most haunting, Doña
Rita, "the harmonized sweetness and daring of whose
face" holds every man and woman in thrall with its fateful beauty. She is not pretty. She is worse, as Mills
tells her. She has the symbolic power of a Mona Lisa
as she sits "tenderly amiable yet somehow distant, among
her cushions, with an immemorial seriousness in her long,
shaded eyes, and her fugitive smile hovering about but

never settling on her lips." "Man is a strange animal,"
writes Monsieur George long afterwards.

> "I didn't care what I said. All I wanted was to
> keep her in her pose, excited and still, sitting up with
> her hair loose, softly glowing, and the dark brown fur
> making a wonderful contrast with the white lace on
> her breast. All I was thinking of was that she was
> adorable and too lovely for words! I cared for noth-
> ing but that sublimely aesthetic impression. It
> summed up all life, all joy, all poetry! It had a
> divine strain."

Here is the symbolic essence of romance.

As perfect is this lyric on Giselle from *Nostromo*.

> "Coppery glints rippled to and fro on the wealth of
> her gold hair. Her smooth forehead had the soft,
> pure sheen of a priceless' pearl in the splendor of the
> sunset, mingling the gloom of starry spaces, the
> purple of the sea, and the crimson of the sky in mag-
> nificent stillness."

It is her voice that best expresses the woman, her
character and her soul. Each man surrenders to its
magic. To Nostromo Giselle speaks "in a voice that re-
called to him the song of running water, the tinkling of
a silver bell." The music of Rita's voice thrills and
fascinates as men listen to its "warm waves" "with a
ripple of badinage," and "its even, mysterious quality."
Heyst is enchanted by Lena's voice. Woman expresses
to Conrad with her voice the

> "Wisdom of the heart, which, having no concern
> with the erection or demolition of theories any more
> than with the defence of prejudices, has no random
> words at its command. The words it pronounces
> have the value of acts of integrity, tolerance and
> compassion."

In their veiled gaze, the inscrutability of their smile, the abstraction of their quietude, all of Conrad's women are emblematic of the mystery of "the incarnation of the feminine," for women and the sea are "the two mistresses of life's values,—the illimitable greatness of the one, and the unfathomable seduction of the other working their immemorial spells from generation to generation,' in "that beautiful world of their own" where men must help them stay lest theirs get worse.

Portraiture is one vehicle of character revelation. It is the expression in technique of that article of Conrad's artistic creed which Ford Madox Hueffer has summarized as "Never comment: state." The first article of that creed, however, Mr. Hueffer says may be epigramatized as "Never state: present." And this is how Conrad renders character through the plot of the story. Every action, every conversation, every recollective remark, brings us one step nearer to an understanding of the man or woman created before us. The chain of happenings is the unfolding of the character of the dramatis personæ.

One incident alone may be a key to the man's whole subsequent conduct. The exasperatingly ludicrous episode of the Siamese flag lays bare before us the character of the sensitive, imaginative Jukes and the stolid, literal-minded Captain MacWhirr. It is what Jim does on board the "Patna" and again in Doramin's campong in Patusan that puts the seal on our knowledge of what his soul is like. It is when Nostromo represses the true story of the treasure and afterwards grows rich slowly that the irony of his self-confident vanity unfolds. It is Doña Rita's visit to Monsieur George's room in his ab-

sence that reveals without disguise her love for him that
we had half doubted till then. It is Lena's supreme act
that is her victory over Heyst's contemptuous negation
of life. It is as Almayer blots out forever Nina's foot-
steps in the sand that our hearts are wrung with "the
anguish of paternity." It is the "horribly merry" glance
of Flora de Barral on that rainy morning when the odious
personage came to drag her back to his impossible household which throws sudden light on her mental state.
The tragedy of Emilia Gould cannot be expressed in act;
therein lies her wretchedness. There is nothing that she
can do. *She* has no silver mine to look after. We must
learn of her unhappiness in one of the rare moments
when she admits us into the hidden reserve of her
thoughts.

Sometimes Conrad pauses in the story to gather together himself all these traits of a character that we have
been watching unfold before us. But he prefers to
postpone such a summary until we are well acquainted
with the men and women themselves, just as in real life
we may stop at some moment to marshal before us all
the known facts in order to comprehend what some one
may do next. The revelation of Mrs. Gould, for instance,
though it occurs a hundred pages from the end of the
long book, is really at the climax of the story. For her
there is nothing more to be said. She must put on a
brave front and face the rest of her life in unspeaking
endurance. The long analysis of Nostromo's character
comes at that crisis in his life when he himself pauses
to review his past success in order to plan his course in

the future,—at the moment when he wakes after his safe swim back to the harbor from the Great Isabel.

But this use of Romantic block summary is rare. Conrad prefers, as we have said, the dramatic method of direct speech and action. Interwoven with this is a painstaking, though apparently casual, rendering of gesture, pose and facial expression so indicative of mood, of personality, and of race. The most vivid instances that come to mind are in *Lord Jim* of the French lieutenant, Stein, old Egström, and of Jim himself. In that study of physiological reactions on which the Realists pride themselves, Conrad shows himself a master. In *Chance, Under Western Eyes, The Secret Agent,* he has taken particular pains to stress this physiological side of Realism. The most elaborate of the descriptions of this sort is the terrible analysis of Winnie Verloc just before and just after she murders her husband.

So real are the people of Conrad's imagination that there is not one of them whom we do not feel that he must at some time in his life have met. Conrad tells us himself that Almayer and Lord Jim were actual men of whom he had caught a glimpse, with whom he had talked. When we read in *A Personal Record* his descriptions of persons whom he knew, we begin to understand his amazing ability to create in fiction living beings, for in this book he has revealed to us the keenness of his observation and the graphic power of his memory. This is his description of the real Almayer, written down twenty-five or more years after Conrad saw him, and recollected from memory only, for Conrad says that he never made

a note of a fact, of an impression, of an anecdote in his
life.

> "I had seen him for the first time, some four years
> before, from the bridge of a steamer, moored to a
> rickety little wharf forty miles up, more or less, a
> Bornean river . . . The forests above and below and
> on the opposite bank looked black and dank; wet
> dripped from the rigging upon the tightly stretched
> deck awnings, and it was in the middle of a shudder-
> ing yawn that I caught sight of Almayer. He was
> moving across a patch of burned grass, in a blurred
> shadowy shape with the blurred bulk of a house be-
> hind him, a low house of mats, bamboos, and palm-
> leaves, with a high pitched roof of grass.
> "He stepped upon the jetty. He was clad simply
> in flapping pajamas of cretonne pattern (enormous
> flowers with yellow petals on a disagreeable blue
> ground) and a thin cotton singlet with short sleeves.
> His arms, bare to the elbow, were crossed on his
> chest. His black hair looked as if it had not been
> cut for a very long time, and a curly wisp of it
> strayed across his forehead . . .
> "He came quite close to the ship's side and raised
> a harrassed countenance, round and flat, with that
> curl of black hair over the forehead and a heavy
> pained glance."

This is a real person to whom through his magic com-
mand over words he is introducing the reader. In his
fictitious characters we find this same actuality of description, based, we feel confident, on personal acquaintance
interpreted through recollective imagination. Here is one
other description which is peculiarly Conradian, the "jolly
skipper of the *Patna*" as Jim sees him on that fatal night.

> "His skipper had come up noiselessly, in pyjamas
> and with his sleeping-jacket flung wide open. Red of
> face, only half awake, the left eye partly closed, the
> right staring stupid and glassy, he hung his big head
> over the chart and scratched his ribs sleepily. There
> was something obscene in the sight of his naked

flesh. His bared breast glistened soft and greasy, as though he had sweated fat in his sleep. He pronounced a professional remark in a voice harsh and dead, resembling the rasping sound of a wood-file on the edge of a plank; the fold of his double chin hung like a bag triced up close under the hinge of his jaw. Jim started, and his answer was full of deference; but the odious and fleshy figure, as though seen for the first time in a revealing moment, fixed itself in his memory for ever as the incarnation of everything vile and base that lurks in the world we love: in our hearts we trust for salvation, in the men that surround us, in the sights that fill our eyes, in the sounds that fill our ears, and in the air that fills our lungs."

In that brief paragraph we have the epitome of Conrad's art:—Realistic photographic detail side by side with the Romantic interpretation of the meaning of things and the yearning for beauty.

PART III

———

ROMANTIC-REALISM IN CONRAD'S USE OF SETTING

THE object of the universe, he would fondly believe, is purely spectacular, Conrad writes in *A Personal Record*. He said the same thing earlier in the Preface to *The Nigger of the Narcissus*:

> "To arrest, for the space of a breath, the hands busy about the work of the earth, and compel men entranced by the sight of distant goals to glance for a moment at the surrounding vision of form and color, of sunshine and shadows; to make them pause for a look, a sigh, for a smile—such is the aim, difficult and evanescent, and reserved only for a very few to achieve. But, sometimes, by the deserving and the fortunate, even that task is accomplished. And when it is accomplished—behold!—all the truth of life is there: a moment of vision, a sigh, a smile— and the return to an eternal rest."

This is war à l'outrance on Stevenson's slogan, "Death to the optic nerve." In a letter of a date ten years previous to the letter to Henry James, in which he expounded this article of his faith, Stevenson had written more fully:

> "The painter must study more from nature than the man of words. But why? Because literature deals with men's business and passions, which in the game of life, we are irresistibly obliged to study; but painting with relations of light, and color, and significances, and form, which from the immemorial habit of the race, we pass over with unregarded eye."

The chief aim of the novelist, in Conrad's opinion, is to make men see these very aspects of life with penetrating and imaginative vision. The intermingling of light and darkness becomes to him the allegory of the known and the unknown in human existence. It is his purpose to make men perceive the sharp reality of the strongly illuminated places, crude and ugly though they may be, and to uplift them by a sense of the mystery of vistas obscured in the half-lights and shadows, or veiled in a mist of beauty and romance. To behold both is to have full vision, to know all the truth of life.

To see life "in its forms, in its colors, in its lights, in its shadows" is to comprehend one of the great words of all time: Beauty.

> "I, who have never sought in the written word anything else but a form of the Beautiful—I have carried over that article of creed from the decks of ships to the more circumscribed space of my desk, and by that act, I suppose, I have become permanently imperfect in the eyes of the ineffable company of esthetes."

Beauty is the symbol to Conrad of "That which is to be contemplated to all Infinity." Through it men approach to understanding of the divine. Little wonder it is then that Conrad's books are flooded with descriptions of color, of light, of shadow, of sound, of persons and of places, of the land, of the sea, and of the sky. It is as a master of description that his power has been most unreservedly proclaimed. There could be no more delightful task than selecting beautiful and representative descriptive passages from his novels and his tales. The difficulty lies in the wealth of choice.

As a writer of the sea he stands supreme:—the sea in serene weather, in dead calm, in tempest and in wind. He makes us know the cold, the heat, the color, the lights of the sea; night and the stars, dawn and the clouds are there; the space and the majesty of the sea, its loneliness, and its unfathomable mystery are there. We perceive it always through the eyes of the men whom it tosses to and fro as midgets in its power, but whose indomitable human spirit it cannot crush.

This ever-varying sea is the back-drop against which move the characters in all of his books; yet some stories he has chosen to be an expression of a sole aspect of the sea. *Typhoon* and *The Nigger of the Narcissus* are among the most tremendously real as well as poetic descriptions of tempest and gale in prose fiction. *The Shadow Line* is the sea in an unearthly calm, a *Rime of the Ancient Mariner* in prose, weird and beautiful, and dreadfully realistic. *Youth* is a lyric of youth and the sea; *The End of the Tether* of the pathos of old age on the sea. Conrad's pictures are more memorable than the events or even the characters themselves in many of these sea stories. They should be read in their entirety, for they are woven into the fabric of the plot.

Boisterous winds and sweeping gales, clear weather, shrouding fog and stifling heat, sunset, moonrise, and the blinding glare of noon fill the pages of Conrad with the vivid pictorial illusion of great marine paintings. His is the art of the etcher, too. The description of the Thames in *Heart of Darkness, The Nigger of the Narcissus, The Secret Agent;* of the harbors in the latter, and in *Lord Jim* of London streets at night and in the

gray light of fog,—might serve as descriptions of
Whistler's etchings.

These pictures are not flat canvasses. Conrad's skill
in the art of language makes real the heat, the cold, the
sound, the motion, the silence, the space of life itself.

As remarkable as his sea pictures are those of the
tropics and the jungle in *Almayer's Folly, An Outcast
of the Islands, Heart of Darkness, Youth, Victory, The
Rescue*. They are painted from actual experience by an
artist of whom might be said the words he wrote of one
of his own characters, "It seems that he had not only a
memory but that he also knew how to remember." Sir
Hugh Clifford, who had been Governor of the Federated
Malay States and had himself written several books about
the Malay, declares that Conrad's "absolute creation"
of the atmosphere of southern Asia is well-nigh perfect.
Every critic of Conrad lays strong emphasis on this romantic—and realistic—picturing of strange, exotic coun-
tries.   In fact, it moves one Mr. Curran to remark that
these scenes of Conrad "beget in us a longing to visit
such quaint corners of the earth!"   This same reviewer
sounds a warning for parents in regard to the Malay
tale *Almayer's Folly*. "This girl Nina, and her Malay
lover," says Mr. Curran, "supply all the amorous and
romantic portions of the story; and, perhaps, it is better
to say in passing that one of these scenes may be thought
by some parents too ardent for young persons to read."

(It is this same gentle critic, by the way, who is
horrified by the corruption spread throughout the South
American republic in Nostromo. "The blooming forth
of that hardy annual Revolution," he says, "is delightfully

done, and one cannot rise from the story without feeling a strong desire to punch the heads of some of its actors. If what the author writes be true, a few good missions would not do Catholicity much harm in the regions south of the United States." There is a naïve tribute to Conrad's realism!)

In *Almayer's Folly*, in *Heart of Darkness*, in *Youth*, the exotic beauty and the rankness of the primeval jungle, the insidious torpor of the tropics, their luxuriance and their decay, are intertwined with every thread of the story, every incident of the plot, and every thought and deed of the characters. Single passages can only suggest the subtle design. It is like fraying out a little thread of an intricately-patterned web to test the color effect of the whole. A few sentences can indicate instantly the demoralizing influence of the land, as in this short paragraph from *Heart of Darkness*:

> "We called at some places with farcical names, where the merry dance of death and trade goes on in a still and earthy atmosphere as of an overheated catacomb; all along the formless coast bordered by dangerous surf, as if Nature herself had tried to ward off intruders; in and out of rivers, streams of death in life, whose banks were rotting into mud, whose waters thickened into slime, invaded the contorted mangroves, that seem to writhe at us in the extremity of an impotent despair. Nowhere did we stop long enough to get a particularized impression, but the general sense of vague and oppressive wonder grew upon me. It was like a weary pilgrimage amongst hints for nightmare."

When the action rises to passion, this tropical exuberance becomes the fit setting for the flaming ruthlessness of love, as in the picture of the forest river on which Dain Maroola met Nina in the early dawn.

It is in his use of setting that Conrad's Romantic-Realism is at once apparent. The all pervading atmosphere is never for the sake of effect alone; it is another of his romantic methods of foreshadowing events and of symbolizing personalities. But this romantic use of background is inextricably associated with his realistic study of the effect of environment on men and women. In *Heart of Darkness*, for example, the unmerciful glare of the African sun, the impenetrable blackness of the jungle, the dank smell of decayed vegetation, the mysterious lure of the impassivity of nature, become first the menace of the land, and then the spell that draws men to "its pitiless breast by the awakening of forgotten and brutal instincts, by the memory of gratified and monstrous passions." Through every description runs this allegorical undertone. The sordidness and desolation of the settlement, and the tangled fecundity of the tropical forests are at once the symbol and the instrument of Almayer's shuffling incompetence and his hopeless tragedy. The sombre tragedy of *The Secret Agent* can be enacted only under a grimy sky, in the dirt of London streets, among the "inhospitable accumulations of bricks, slates and stones—things in themselves unlovely and unfriendly to man," where the perpetual fog and rain and mud steep every beautiful thing in their own sodden atmosphere. "And the lofty pretensions of a mankind oppressed by the miserable indignities of the weather appeared as a colossal and hopeless vanity deserving of scorn, wonder and compassion." At one point in this book the weather is definitely accessory to the action. Had not the boat-train been practically empty on account of the time of the year and the abominable weather, Winnie Verloc might have been noticed by a fellow passenger, might have been questioned, or might have found some understanding soul to unburden herself to, and her fate might have been less tragic.

The general harmony between the setting and the sinister nature of the plot in this novel becomes in places manifestly suggestive of what is to come. This is a matter of style, to be sure.   When Winnie Verloc plunges into the street in search of help, we read,

> "She floundered over the doorstep head forward, arms thrown out, like a person falling over the parapet of a bridge. This entrance into the open air had a foretaste of drowning; a shiny dampness enveloped her, entered her nostrils, clung to her hair."

Every phrase in the passage connotes her future fate.

Likewise in *Lord Jim* choice of words can make us prescient of the future, as we read of the voyage of the "Patna" over the burning, still Arabian sea, "'viscous, stagnant, dead." She passes on "with a slight hiss," "smouldering in a luminous immensity, as if scorched by a flame flicked at her from heaven without pity."

In *Nostromo* the careful description in the Prelude of the mountains, the coastline, the harbor, and the city,— sky, land and sea, the sinister veil of overhanging cloud, close in ominously the action of the whole story until, ironically, on human anguish "the moonlight in the offing closed as if with a colossal bar of silver the entrance of the Placid Gulf—the sombre cavern of clouds and stillness in the surf-fretted seaboard."

In *The Arrow of Gold,* in striking contrast to the exuberant descriptions of the earlier books, there are only three descriptions of nature, all of them of the briefest, hardly more than five or six lines long; yet in this novel, too, we realize that the weather is symbolic. This one adventurous year of Monsieur George's life opens and closes on the cold blasts of the mistral that leave him shivering and desolate.

In his last novel *The Rescue* Conrad has returned to his earlier romantic method of evoking through the magic of his style that tropical setting which shapes the destinies of the beings caged within its enchanted bounds. Edith Travers expresses the symbolism of the background of the story as she looks across the lagoon at the edge of the forest.

"That great erection of enormous solid trunks, dark, rugged columns festooned with writhing creepers and steeped in gloom, was so close to the bank that by looking over the side of the ship she could see inverted in the glassy belt of water its massive and black reflection on the reflected sky that gave the impression of a clear blue abyss seen through a transparent film. And when she raised her eyes the same abysmal immobility seemed to reign over the whole sun-bathed enlargement of that lagoon which was one of the secret places of the earth. She felt strongly her isolation. She was so much the only being of her kind moving within this mystery that even to herself she looked like an apparition without rights and without defense and that must end by surrendering to those forces which seemed to her but the unconscious genius of the place. Hers was the most complete loneliness charged with a catastrophic tension. It lay about her as though she had been set apart within a magic circle. It cut off—but it did not protect."

Lingard's happiness, like the dazzling color and flaming
light of the islands and seas of the Shore of Refuge, is
swallowed up in an intense black pall that closes in on
the world in such a silence that "one might have fancied
oneself come to the end of time."

The greatest achievement of all these studies in background is *Nostromo*. The book leaves us with an
ineradicable impression of having actually lived in Sulaco.
With Emilia Gould we have traveled through the ravines
and across the plains of Costaguana, over the long, dusty,
hot roads at the foot of the snow-covered Sierra, past the
pueblos and the estates, the smooth-walled haciendas, till
we turned from the broad Campo to Sulaco itself lying
in the curve of the hushed Placid Gulf. We have driven
past the harbor with its wooden jetties and moored ships,
through the slums to the custom-house and the new iron-
roofed railway station, down the Alameda, dotted with
family coaches of the "best families" of Sulaco, over to
the market-place where in the morning the peasant
women spread their umbrellas over fruit and flower
stands, and in the evening cooked their meals over the
red coals of the brazeros glowing in the dark, past
churches and cathedral, past shops and cafés, to the
shuttered houses of the residence section where we taste
"the worn-out antiquity of the old town, so characteristic
with its stuccoed houses and barred windows, with the
great yellowy-white walls of abandoned convents behind
the rows of sombre green cypresses." As "the bells of
the city were striking the hour of Oracion," the carriage
has rolled under the old gateway of the Casa Gould, and
like Decoud we turn to contemplate the inner aspect of

the gate. No wonder, we think, that Mrs. Gould loved the patio of her Spanish house as we watch her standing below the painting of the blue-robed Madonna with the crowned child in her arms, looking down through the leaves and flowers of the rows of shading plants between the arches on the high balustrade to the paved quadrangle below where slender bamboo stems drooped over the cistern, and the busy life of the Spanish household went to and fro in sunlight and shadow beneath her quiet gaze. Both the countryside and the city teem with life. Aristocrats, caballeros, officers, merchants, cargadores, peasants, laborers, beggars, burdened Indians, Italians and Occidentals, and picturesque Spaniards, incorrigible in their light-heartedness and in their brutality, dancing one day, rioting the next, fighting tumultuously in violent revolution, placid and passionate by turns,—all throng past us and around us like a spectacle of life itself. In what other novel is a whole country so convincingly created!

The descriptions in Conrad, however poetic they may be, always keep touch with reality through some minuteness of detail in sharp contrast with the previous picturesqueness of the scene, or through alternate successions of Romantic and Realistic methods. For example, the serenity of the sunset glow, reflected down the middle of the main thoroughfare of the Eastern port, falls on the brilliant costumes and brown and yellow faces of the turbaned Indian crowd and on the gay parasols in the slow-moving procession of European carriages, touches with rosy light the dark-blue curve of the quiet bay, and flames fiercely on a prosaic tightly-packed street car

which "in a red haze of dust navigated cautiously up the
human stream with the incessant blare of its horn, in the
manner of a steamer groping in a fog."

As in life, sublime and commonplace mingle. With
the smouldering hull of their fire-gutted ship crackling
and roaring beneath them, the crew of the "Judea" calmly
sit down to an improvised meal of bread and cheese and
bottled stout while the blazing sheet of fire shoots tongues
of flame behind and above them. In the silence of the
sleeping camp on the moonlit plateau high among the
peaks of the Sierra where the white Higuerota "soared
out of the shadows of rock and earth like a frozen bubble
under the moon," a pack-mule stamped his forefoot
and blew heavily twice. As the furious gale buffets the
huddled crew of the "Narcissus,"

> "a fierce squall seemed to burst asunder the thick
> mass of sooty vapours; and above the wrack of torn
> clouds glimpses could be caught of the high moon
> rushing backwards with frightful speed over the sky,
> right in the wind's eye. Many hung their heads,
> muttering that it 'turned their inwards out' to look at
> it. Soon the clouds closed up, and the world again
> became a raging, blind darkness that howled, flinging
> at the lonely ship salt sprays and sleet."

The sudden impact of the contrast brings you up with
a shock as in this description of the inspired cook of the
"Narcissus," when after being carried away on the flood
of his religious fervor, we see him through James Wait's
eyes.

> "The cook's lips moved inaudibly; his face was
> rapt, his eyes turned up. He seemed to be mentally
> imploring deck beams, the brass hook of the lamp,
> two cockroaches."

Sometimes the glamour fades entirely and only the sordid remains, as in the description of Schomberg's squalid and hot hotel, or of the filthy tenement inn that harbored the teeming misery of Russia's slums where fate played a trumpcard in Razumov's destiny, or in the photographic detail of Verloc's shabby shop.

It may be objected that these examples of Realistic detail are all of unpleasant things. But it is for the unpleasant that Conrad reserves this method; the beautiful are depicted with the color and suggestiveness of Romanticism, with the mystery, that "fascination of the incomprehensible" for which all men yearn and which the simple minds of the big children of the sea find in the pages of undiluted, romantic novels of adventure, that stir them by the

> "enigmatical disclosure of a resplendent world that exists with the frontier of infamy and filth, within that border of dirt and hunger, of misery and dissipation, that comes down on all sides to the water's edge of the incorruptible ocean, and is the only thing they know of life, the only thing they see of land,—those life-long prisoners of the sea. Mystery!"

This is that romance which Marlow heard in the low voice of Kurtz' beloved, which seemed

> "to have the accompaniment of all other sounds, full of mystery, desolation, and sorrow, I had ever heard—the ripple of the river, the soughing of the trees swayed by the wind, the murmurs of wild crowds, the faint ring of incomprehensible words cried from afar, the whisper of a voice speaking from beyond the threshold of an eternal darkness."

So is Romance the core of Reality.

Among the romantic qualities of Conrad is his love of color. His descriptions are as colorful as the poems

of Rossetti and Keats or as luminous as Shelley's, and the
language as poetical.   Red, blue, gold, silver, black,
purple, gleam in all the pictures like pure color on a
painter's canvas.   He loves the glow of sunset over land
and sea when "tints of purple, gold and crimson" are
"mirrored in the clear water of the harbor," and the
waves toss red sparks on the sandy beaches, when
mountain and island and coastline lengthen in softened
outlines, purple-black, against the flaming magnificence of
the sky.   He paints the brilliant blue of the sea, sparkling
in sunshine, the gold and silver of the rising moon and
veiling clouds, and the moon's path on the flowing black
waves.   He has Corot's fondness for a point of red in
the picture, whether it be the red of dress or hood, the
crimson of a scarf, the bronze gleams of a woman's hair,
the glow of a fire burning in the darkness, the glory of a
flaming sunset reflected on cloud or on the sails of ships,
or the flaming red of the British ensign.

But an attentive reader of Conrad cannot fail to
observe that he paints the greater number of his scenes
in chiaroscuro.   The brilliance of unshaded sunlight
gives way to the softer splendor of one focus of
light, narrowed in by masses of obscuring blacks
and browns.   We find vast shadows, dark laid on
dark, out of which dim shapes emerge in grayish
gloom, or stand out clearly modeled in sharp gleams
of yellow and red light:—flame in the night; shafts
of sunlight across a darkened room or the glow of
a torch in a dim street; lamp or candlelight illuminating
a shadowed face or room or ship's deck in the night;
sunset splendor fading to enveloping dusk; the jewelled

points of the lights of a city along a black horizon line;
clear patches of sun in the surrounding sombreness of
dark forest; indistinct figures silhouetted in the moonlight
or the transparent semi-darkness of a starry night;
dazzling light in a cloudy sky; white-crested waves in
the solid blackness of an inky sea. There are long
galleries of such pictures as these. To take only one
example, there is pure poetry in the description of night
on the "Narcissus," nights on which Donkin prowled,
spiteful and plotting evil.

> "On clear evenings, the silent ship, under the cold
> sheen of the dead moon, took on the false aspect of
> passionless repose resembling the winter of the earth.
> Under her a long band of gold barred the black disc
> of the sea. Footsteps echoed on her quiet decks.
> The moonlight clung to her like a frosted mist and
> the white sails stood out in dazzling cones as of stain-
> less snow. In the magnificence of the phantom rays,
> the ship appeared pure like a vision of ideal beauty,
> illusive like a tender dream of serene peace. And
> nothing in her was real, nothing was distinct and
> solid but the heavy shadows that filled her decks
> with their unceasing and noiseless stir; the shadows
> blacker than the night and more restless than the
> thoughts of men."

This play of light on shadow is more than mere picturesque ornament to the story. Underlying it is the
allegory which makes of it a column in the structure of
the plot. At times this allegory is implied; but its inner
significance Conrad has consciously made clear more than
once. We should understand that in *Heart of Darkness*
the contrast of light and darkness symbolizes the theme
of the story even if Marlow had not taken the trouble to
explain in his tone, half grim, half jesting, that he
was sent as "something like an emissary of light" into

the land that seemed to beckon with "a treacherous appeal
to the lurking death, to the hidden evil, to the profound
darkness of its heart."   Not alone the sinister gleam of
the silver clouds above the impenetrable obscurity of the
Golfo Placido carries an allegorical meaning; we understand the sadder human effort of Emilia Gould to
withstand the encroaching darkness of material interests
in such an apparently unportentous sentence as this:
"Only the sala of the Casa Gould flung out defiantly the
blaze of its four windows, the bright appeal of light in
the whole dumb obscurity of the street."

As Almayer watches the yellow triangle of the prau
shine brilliantly on the blue of the open sea till it vanishes
in the shadow of the headline, we know with him, unmis-
takably, that it is the disappearing emblem of his own
happiness.   The yellow gleam of the riding-light in the
fore-rigging burns as a symbolic flame to guide the Secret
Sharer to that ship where accident and fate have awaiting
him the one narrow ray of light out of his darkness,—the
man who will understand and help him.   In *Under
Western Eyes* the snow-covered land of Russia stretching
vast and white into the obscurity of surrounding night is
"like a monstrous blank page awaiting the record of an
inconceivable history."   To it Razumov likens his own
cold, blank existence.   What irony lies in the focus of
light on Mrs. Verloc's wedding ring after she has just
learned the truth of Steevie's death, or on the flash of
jewels and gold of the many rings on Mrs. Gould's white
hands as she drops them wearily into her lap!

Life, Conrad says, is altogether "the brilliance of sunshine together with the unfathomable splendor of the

night." There had been no path in his life until he knew
love for Rita, says Monsieur George in *The Arrow of
Gold*. At the end of *Heart of Darkness* Marlow had
said the same thing.

Love and faith alone illumine the impenetrable
obscurity of human existence. They shine radiantly in
the surrounding darkness. Will they eternally endure?
That, too, is inscrutable, says Conrad. To the eyes of
men it would seem that even they can grow dim and fade
away. "But not for long!"*

* "The Arrow of Gold," page 138.

PART IV

The Spirit of Conrad

THE fusion of light and darkness embodies Conrad's attitude toward life. In fact, more than once, he puts this parable of life into the mouth of Marlow. Not only in *Heart of Darkness* but also in *Lord Jim*, Marlow uses the figure repeatedly. He reads into the obscuring physical shadows and lights that surround Jim an interpretation of the inexplicable that perpetually crosses the light of our understanding of human character and of existence itself. "If there were no dark places, no shadows, no half-lights, would men's dim comprehension be illumined in the full radiance that would reveal all?" Conrad seems to question. "But light," he answers, "comes in flashes only, and in flashes only is revelation made clear." This is the dominant strain in Conrad: an abiding realization of the mystery that shrouds life. He does not solve the mystery. He presents it as it is. All we can look for are the gleams of understanding that will irradiate the dimness.

Because Conrad never sentimentalizes over the inscrutability of life, because he presents it with clear-eyed comprehension of what it involves, he has been accused by his reviewers of being both pessimist and cynic. There is Mr. Mencken, for instance, whose admiration of

74

Conrad is based on what he considers an obvious similarity of temperament. He makes Conrad out to have the same misogynic and disillusioned attitude toward life to which he has himself attained, and savagely commends his pessimism.

> "In the midst of futile meliorism, which deceives the more it soothes, he (Conrad) stands out like some sinister skeleton at the feast, regarding the festivities with a flickering and impenetrable grin."

Arthur Symons is equally convinced of Conrad's "sullen subjective vision." "Conrad's inexplicable mind," he says,

> "has created for itself a secret world to live in, some corner stealthily hidden away from view, among impenetrable forests, on the banks of untravelled rivers. From that corner, like a spider in his web, he throws out tentacles into the darkness; he gathers in his spoils, he collects them like a miser, stripping from them their dreams and visions to decorate his web magnificently . . . Beyond and below this obscure realm, beyond and below human nature itself, Conrad is seen through the veil of the persons of his drama, living a hidden, exasperated life."

Such statements (and there are other critics who accuse him of this bitter cynicism), would lead the reader to believe that Conrad is nothing but a grim Realist, laying bare the inconsistencies, faults, and vices of mankind with an exultant flash of his dissecting knife as he uncovers each putrid spot. But it is at this point of union with the Realistic school that Conrad steps aside into his own personality. He himself has asserted that all art is revealed through the personality of the artist himself.

> "I know that a novelist lives in his work. He stands there, the only reality in an invented world,

among imaginary things, happenings, and people.
Writing about them, he is only writing about himself.
But the disclosure is not complete. He remains, to
a certain extent, a figure behind the veil; a suspected,
rather than a seen presence—a movement and a voice
behind the draperies of fiction."*

Conrad's personality, as he reveals it in his books, is
not that of the disillusioned materialist. His stories, to
be sure, lack that exuberance of sheer glory in living that
emanates from the hearty spirit of the Romancer.
His books are never joyous; they leave you always
thoughtful, sometimes even depressed. His is the
humor of the serious man. We never find him
joining in the merriment, and creating it for others.
He stands aside as the observer. His eyes smile,
but he seldom laughs outright. The only unreflectively
funny incident in any of his books is the landing of
Almayer's pony in *A Personal Record;* but that passage
alone is sufficient to refute the assertion that Conrad has
no humor. It is a delicious fragment of pure comedy,—
and full of sympathy with the pony. But this is the
only instance of open drollery in Conrad. *The Duel,* to
be sure, is a comedy tale, but it is fantastic and whimsical
rather than broadly funny. His humor is of a kind more
subtle than good-natured jollity. In the perception of
inexplicable and omnipresent incongruities Conrad sees
manifested the all-enveloping mystery of life.

You may explain a man's character by the careful
analysis of his racial heredity and of his physical and
social environment. You may see that he reacts according to understood psychological laws. Conrad does this

* "A Personal Record," page 4.

in every one of his stories, as I have endeavored to show. Almayer, Kurtz, Razumov, Heyst, Charles Gould, Decoud, Singleton, Donkin—many others—are all formed out of tendencies inherited from their social ancestry and shaped by the forces of their surroundings. Conrad omits no word nor deed nor bit of description which shall make this explicit. Yet character evolution is not so mechanistic as this; it would be too much like putting men and women into the glass jars of a biological laboratory, labeled as specimens. To such precise scientific reconstruction of human character, there is a power in destiny, which (to paraphrase) declares: "Hitherto shalt thou come, but no further; and here shall thy proud laws be stayed." We perceive, like Marlow, "how incomprehensible, wavering, and misty are the beings that share with us the sight of the stars and the warmth of the sun." It is this mysterious element in character and in life in which Conrad is absorbed.

It manifests itself, first of all, in the incalculable. Things turn out so contrary to all expectation. Jim and the officers of the "Patna" had every reason to believe that the rotten bulkhead would give way any instant; but it held out after all. Almayer thought that he was furthering his plans for a happy future with Nina when he took Dain Maroola as his confederate; but Nina loved the Malay chief, and Almayer fell in with bitter anguish. Verloc supposed that Steevie would be an innocent, unscathed tool to his careful plot; but Steevie stumbled. Ned and Charley congratulated themselves that at last the dire spell of the Brute, *The Apse Family*, was broken; and in the very moment of their exultation the most unlooked-for kind of dreadful accident happened. Emilia Gould joined enthusiastically in her husband's plans to use the San Tomé mine as a means to rehabilitate Sulaco, and Charles Gould proved its slave, and her happiness was ruined.

These unexpected turns of fate are the tragic irony of human existence. Destiny lies hid to play her wanton tricks in ordering the affairs of men. Chance is her handmaid. De Barral might just as well have engaged a perfectly harmless usual specimen of governess for his daughter, but "chance being incalculable" he fell upon that vulgar-minded woman who nearly ruined Flora's life. It was chance that brought Flora and Captain Anthony together. It was the supreme chance that young Powell stooped to pick up a coil of rope left lying on the deck by some one's carelessness, and so brought his head down to the level of the after skylight at the moment when that fatal, senile hand was thrust between the curtains of the Captain's cabin. It was chance that left the rope ladder hanging over the side of the ship in *The Secret Sharer*. It was chance—or fatality—that led Heyst to Schomberg's hotel at Bangkok on the night when Zangiacomo's Ladies' Orchestra was established there. It was chance —or fatality—that Ziemianitch should have been steeped in a sodden, drunken sleep so that Razumov could not wake him even by a brutal beating. Examples are too many to enumerate at length. Things happen by chance.

It may have been the strange chances in his own career that led Conrad to perceive with lucidity the manifest part that accident plays in life. The most tremendous phenomenon of all the obscure, hidden forces at work

in his own life, he says, was the writing of the first page
of *Almayer's Folly*.

"From the moment I had, in the simplicity of my
heart and the amazing ignorance of my mind, written
that page, the die was cast. Never had Rubicon been
more blindly forded, without invocation to the gods,
without fear of men."

Moreover, he asserts if he had not got to know Almayer
pretty well, it is almost certain there would never have
been a line of his in print. Thus a chance meeting with
an unknown foreigner in a remote Malay settlement on
the East Coast turned Conrad from Master Mariner to
Master Writer.

Such happenings as these are outside the control or the
planning of the men and women whose destinies they
shape. Stranger still are the unaccountable acts of men.
A man never knows himself when he thinks about himself; his deeds are his measure. And fáte is sure to put
him to that test which will knock his self-assurance to
atoms. Jim was romantically certain beforehand of his
shining courage in face of emergency. Taken unawares,
he did the preposterously inconceivable thing. The fugitive in *The Secret Sharer* had found out suddenly that
there lurked in his nature incredible impulses that brought
forth uncalculated action. Falk's abhorrence of himself
afterwards could not wipe out for him the fact that he
had once eaten human flesh. In the face of temptation
Nostromo's incorruptible fidelity crumbled to dusty ashes.
Until Haldin startled him in his rooms that winter day,
Razumov had not dreamed himself capable of acting a
Brutus' part.

It is Razumov, in fact, who is the most mystically im-

pressed with the strangeness of life: the secret places, the
secret influences over a man's thoughts, the surprises of
life, astonishing impulses, mysterious motives of conduct.
"A man's most open actions have a secret side to them.
That is interesting and so unfathomable!" he contends
to Haldin. Conrad says of himself that he could not
explain his own determined resolve to become an English
seaman. He could not understand the mysteriousness of
his own impulses.

> "I understood no more than the people who called
> upon me to explain myself. There was no precedent.
> I verily believe mine was the only case of a boy of
> my nationality and antecedents taking a, so to speak,
> standing jump out of his racial surroundings and
> associations."

Another of the incomprehensible aspects of life to
which Conrad draws our attention is the disparity between men's deserts and their destinies. Five times out
of ten poetic justice is an ideal of the sentimentalist rather
than the experience in reality, he affirms. It is the
women and the simple-hearted who suffer most unfairly
in Conrad's books. Emilia Gould, Antonia Avellanos,
Linda Viola, Natalie Haldin suffer beyond anything they
have merited. We leave them to sorrow who have de-
served great joy. Harmless, half-witted Steevie, the for-
lorn outcast whom Amy Foster married, and Flora de
Barral, even Doña Rita, are victims of circumstance.
The men who do wrong usually pay for it, as do Razumov, and Verloc, and Kurz; and the villains sometimes
meet a fitting end, as do Riccardo and Jones. But even
the sinners often pay a heavier penalty in suffering than
their deeds would justly warrant. Doctor Monygham,

Captain Whalley, Heyst, Lord Jim, Almayer are weak not wicked; yet they suffer as much and pay as sternly for breach of faith with their fellowmen and with life, as those who have committed deliberated crimes.   It even happens that bad men and women come off unscathed. Flora's evil governess, Donkin, Schomberg, the second mate in *Typhoon*, are about as well off at the end of the tale as they were in the beginning.

Notwithstanding these perversions of justice, Conrad holds no brief for cynicism.   Those who call him cynic have misread the purpose of his work.   "Cynicism seems to me a word invented by hypocrites," Marlow says; and in this instance, assuredly, Marlow and Conrad are one.

No.   Conrad's aim is to show up evil and reveal goodness.   Though he can "see the hog in Nature" and delineate it with acid strokes of his pen, it is not that for which he is searching.   Human nature is not perfect, even in the best, he shows.   But it is the striving for the things that are worth while in spiritual evaluation that makes a man or woman admirable.   Fine qualities are instinctive, Conrad seems to say; for it is in the simplest natures that we find them unadulterated.   The more primitive a man is, the more sterling his worth.   Imagination stultifies; it is the "enemy of man," as Jim discovers.   *The Nigger of the Narcissus* holds a thesis for this very point. Old Singleton, strong, unthinking, inarticulate, enduring, faithful, is the epic personification of fundamental virtues.   It is not in the fine linen of men that Conrad is interested.   He can confess quizzically with Marlow

"in each case all I could see was merely the human being.   A confounded democratic quality of vision

which may be better than total blindness, but has
been of no advantage to me, I can assure you. Men
expect one to take into account their fine linen. But
I could never get up any enthusiasm about these
things. Oh! It's a failing; it's a failing."

Though to the finical, Singleton is only a "poor bibulous
old salt," as Mr. Curran calls him; though when he came
unsteadily up to make his mark on the payroll, he was
"uncertain as to daylight, and brown drops of tobacco
juice maculated his white beard," yet it is venerable
Singleton, steadfast and uncomplaining in his duty, and
little Belfast, the loyal, who won the universal respect
of the crew. Evil made them uneasy, but they were not
completely contaminated by it. The nigger's tacit
demand on their pity which he disdained, his ostentatious
assumption of their subservience, his frightened denial of
death, upset and demoralized them. "Falsehood
triumphed," but they distrusted it. Donkin, the sneak,
and the whiner, they were men enough to judge and cast
out with stony looks when it came to the test.

To Conrad the sea is the place of the true peace of God.
Envy and greed have their domain on land. The "foolish
noise of turbulent mankind," its selfishness and sordid
anxiety, emanates from the discontented land like an
impure breeze, like a tremulous and begriming vapor.
How Marlow hates the cities! "I found myself back in
the sepulchral city," he says one time, "resenting the
sight of people hurrying through the streets to filch a
little money from each other, to devour their infamous
cookery, to gulp their unwholesome beer, to dream their
insignificant and silly dreams." Powell, grown older,
ascribes the "universal inefficiency of what he called the

'shore-gang' to "the want of responsibility and to a sense of security." The service of the sea, on the other hand, is "invested with an elemental moral beauty by the absolute straight-forwardness of its appeal and by the singleness of its purpose." It protects and consoles men.

Through sordid and sublime intermingle in the strange scheme of life, though destiny appear incomprehensible and all men weak, though all visible things pass by, and the meaning of nothing shines clear, yet man is a spiritual being. Even the weakest is ennobled by glorious aspirations.

The earliest of these is the glamour of youth. Although Conrad has outgrown any illusions of his own, he understands that illusion pervades the beginning of life. *Youth* and *The Shadow Line* when read in sequence show how completely Conrad comprehends the magic of youth and the backward glance of the man who has crossed through experience the shadow line into manhood. Illusion may go; but once it has been; and there is nothing equal to the power of it.

When the disenchantment comes, as come it must, what then? In this practical world a man becomes a man when he puts away childish illusions. "Charles Gould was competent because he had no illusions." When it comes about that a man has lost the thrill of adventure and the zest for a world seen through the eyes of youth, then he must put his hand to his work. Work is the saving power in life, Marlow urges again and again: not just doing something, but real accomplishment which will count as the expression of a man's own personality, work in which he can find himself. "What does the price matter if the trick be well done?" It is the spirit in which the work is undertaken that counts,—"an honest concern for the right way of going to work." Though we have to "pick our way in crosslights," we trust that

> "we shall manage yet to go out decently in the end
> —but not so sure of it after all—and with dashed
> little help to expect from those we touch elbows with
> right and left."

But action, Conrad avers, is consolatory. "It is the enemy of thought and the friend of flattering illusions. Only in the conduct of our action can we find the sense of mastery over the Fates." It is in putting our best into that work which "obeys the particular earnestness of our temperament" that we taste the comfort of a finer illusion—the belief in our own worth.

With work must be faith, a deliberate belief in truth. Mere principles are not enough; for they may go to smash in the crucial moment, as Jim and Razumov and the others found. The restraining influences of ordered society, "the holy terror of scandal and gallows and lunatic asylums" are not enough; for a man must be a man when they no longer surround him. Therein, Almayer and Wilhelms and Kurtz failed. Lingard reflects "that in truth and courage there is found wisdom." Strength lies in holding fast to truth, and truth is goodness. It is of the spirit. Idealists, like Lena and Emilia Gould, may be crushed by unconscious or deliberate materialism, but the victory is theirs, for they have realized the truth. Sincerity, unselfishness, sympathy, love, are the truth of life. Courage, endurance, responsibility, fidelity to duty, are the ethics on which the solidarity of mankind is

founded. It is in the fellowship of these primal virtues
that the strength of mankind lies.

> "Those who read me know my conviction that the
> world, the temporal world, rests on a few very simple
> ideas; so simple that they must be as old as the
> hills. It rests, notably, among others, on the idea of
> Fidelity."

So Conrad declares in his preface to *A Personal Record*.
Through the sympathetic understanding of other people,
Marlow thinks,

> "there springs in us compassion, charity, indigna-
> tion, the sense of solidarity; and in minds of any
> largeness an inclination to that indulgence which is
> next door to affection."

Because the men of the sea are held in strong bonds
by the fellowship of the craft, because they are shut
away from "the vanities and errors of a world which
follows no severe rule," by the exacting life of the sea
which knits together a ship's company in courage, endurance, faith, and loyalty, Conrad finds in sailors the highest
type of this fundamental brotherhood of mankind.
Sailors more than any other group of men face every
moment of their lives the immensity of an unconcerned
Nature. All men are equal before it. To the seaman
the sea is " the mistress of his existence and more inscrutable than Destiny." Its "glittering surface and light-
less depths" become to him the symbol of life. At times
it is a cruel and relentless monster, heartless in its mali-
cious attempts to crush the insignificant atoms who defy
its terrible might. The gale torments them, the sun and
the stars stare pitilessly aloof. Man is perpetually sur-
rounded by "the immense indifference of things." The

more honor to him, then, for his indomitable endurance,
and the ardor of his high endeavor.   The Dark Powers
"always on the verge of triumph are perpetually foiled by
the steadfastness of men."   It is in their steadfast perse-
verance and their belief that loyalty, duty, obedience, service, endure in the race of men, that alien is knit to alien,
nation to nation in a common kinship of passion, of in-
domitability and of aspiration.   It might have been of
Joseph Conrad's achievement in literature that Mr.
Woodberry wrote these words:

> "Idealism . . . is in a sense a glorification of the
> commonplace. Its realism lies in the common lot of
> men; its distinction is to embrace truth for all, and
> truth in its universal forms of experience and person-
> ality, the primary, elementary, equally shared fates,
> passions, beliefs of the race."

But small proportion of all that Conrad has written is
devoted to giving us information about his views on these
matters.   Instead he makes us acquainted with the things
themselves through the stories of individual men and
women who have upheld or denied them by the manner of
their lives.   Conrad has twice distinctly denied that he
has any direct moral purpose: once, in the "Preface" to
The Nigger of the Narcissus, and again in "A Familiar
Preface" to *A Personal Record.*   He has no desire, he
says, to reprove, to flatter, or to teach mankind.   Art,
not morality, is his aim.   His task is to make men see
life.   His expression of the great spectacle becomes, then,
of supreme importance to him.

Because he sees actuality, he would make us see it too.
It is only through his expression that he can do this.
Style thus becomes identical with method.   For that

knowledge of life which is objective and intellectual, he uses the method of photographic accuracy of detail, of analysis, of logical synthesis, which demands keen eyes and impersonal recording—the method of Realism, in other words. He gives to his observation precision through the use of concrete words, telling phrases, concise sentences. There is no flowing melody here, but sharp, staccato measures. On the other hand, for that knowledge which is intuitive, not based on fact, knowledge which transcends objective experience—all that knowledge which he himself includes in the great word Mystery!— for this he employs the style of the Romanticist. Symbolism shadows it forth, and beauty is its shining light. Therefore he makes use of connotative words, of assonance, of rhythm, of fluent sentences, and of the refrain of repeated phrases. It is in his metaphors of light and darkness woven like delicate patterns through the fabric of the tales, but above all in his descriptions of the sea that we hear this subtle and suggestive music. Conrad does not hesitate, indeed, to write pure poetry. The idyll of Nostromo and Giselle, the glory of Monsieur George's love for Rita, the coming of the dawn to Nina and Dain Marooia, the moonrise over the "Patna," are all of them lyrics.

In all that Conrad has written, the outlines of his sharply intense Realism are blurred by the softening shades of his Romanticism, blending like the mingled light and gloom of his own favorite allegory of this tenebrous life of ours. What he said of one of his own characters, he might well have written of himself;

> "He appealed to all sides at once,—to the side turned perpetually to the light of day, and to that side of us, which, like the other hemisphere of the moon, exists stealthily in perpetual darkness, with only a fearful ashy light falling at times on the edge."

and his own "imperishable reality" comes to us

> "with a convincing, an irresistible force . . . as though in our progress amongst fleeting gleams of light and the sudden revelations of human figures stealing with flickering flames within unfathomable and pellucid depths we had appproached nearer to absolute Truth, which, like Beauty itself, floats elusive, obscure, half submerged, in the silent still waters of mystery."

APPENDICES

APPENDICES

I. BIBLIOGRAPHIES

1920. A BIBLIOGRAPHY OF THE WRITINGS OF JOSEPH
CONRAD (1895-1920). By Thomas J. Wise. London:
Printed for Private Circulation Only by Richard Clay
& Sons, Ltd. 1920.
This is the most recent bibliography on Conrad, and
the most complete. It is compiled primarily for col-
lectors of first editions of Conrad's works.

1917. JOSEPH CONRAD:, A CONTRIBUTION TOWARD A
BIBLIOGRAPHY. Compiled by Sara W. Eno, Refer-
ence Librarian, Bryn Mawr College, in "Bulletin of
Bibliography," Vol. 9, No. 6, April, 1917.
This is a very complete bibliography. It contains also
a bibliography of book reviews in current periodicals.

1912. BIBLIOGRAPHIES OF YOUNGER REPUTATIONS:
JOSEPH CONRAD. By Vincent Sanger, in "The
Bookman," 35:70, March, 1912.
This is not complete, and extends only through the
year of its publication, 1912.

1914. Appendix to Richard Curle's book, JOSEPH CONRAD,
A STUDY. New York: Doubleday, 1914.
This is only a list of Conrad's works up to 1914.

1915. Appendix to Hugh Walpole's book, JOSEPH CONRAD.
London: Nisbet & Co., Ltd., 1915. New York: Holt,
1915.
This also contains only a list of Conrad's works.

II. CONRAD'S WORKS

A. *Chronological List of Novels and Tales*
(With Original Editions)

1895. ALMAYER'S FOLLY: A STORY OF AN EASTERN
RIVER. London: Unwin, 1895. N. Y.: Macmillan,
1895.

1896. AN OUTCAST OF THE ISLANDS
London: Unwin, 1896. N. Y.: Appleton, 1896.

1898. THE NIGGER OF THE NARCISSUS: A TALE OF
THE SEA. London: Heinemann, 1898. N. Y.: Dodd,
Mead, 1898 (1897?) under title "Children of the Sea:
A Tale of the Forecastle." N. Y.: Doubleday, 1914,
under English title.
(Appeared as a Serial in "The New Review," August
to December, 1897.)

1898. TALES OF UNREST.
London, Unwin, 1898. N. Y., Scribner, 1898.
Contents: KARAIN (1897); THE IDIOTS (1898); AN
OUTPOST OF PROGRESS; THE RETURN; THE
LAGOON (1897).
See List of Short Stories.

1900. LORD JIM: A ROMANCE
London: Blackwood's, 1900. N. Y.: Doubleday, 1900.
(Appeared as a serial in "Blackwood's," December,
1899 to November, 1900.)

1901. THE INHERITORS: AN EXTRAVAGANT STORY
(In collaboration with Ford Madox Hueffer.)
London: Heinemann, 1901. N. Y.: McClure, Phillips,
1901.

1902. YOUTH: A NARRATIVE, AND TWO OTHER STOR-
IES. London: Blackwood's, 1902. N. Y.: McClure,
Phillips, 1903.

1902. YOUTH was published in "Blackwood's Magazine" in September, 1898 and then serially in "The Critic" February to May, 1902.

1899. HEART OF DARKNESS was published serially in "Blackwood's," February to April, 1899.

1902. THE END OF THE TETHER was published serially in "Blackwood's," July to December, 1902.

1902. TYPHOON.
London: Heinemann, 1903. N. Y.: Putnam, 1902.
(Appeared as a serial in "Pall Mall" Magazine, January to March 1902.)
Translated into French by André Gide in "Revue de Paris," March 1, 1918—March 15, 1918.

1903. FALK: AMY FOSTER: TOMORROW. (Three Stories)
N. Y.: McClure, Phillips & Co., 1903.
See List of Short Stories.

1903. ROMANCE: A NOVEL. (In collaboration with Ford Madox Hueffer.)
London: Smith Elder, 1903. N. Y.: McClure, Phillips, 1904.

1904. NOSTROMO: A TALE OF THE SEABOARD.
London: Harper, 1904. N. Y. Harper, 1904.
(Appeared as a serial in "T. P.'s Weekly," January 29 to October 7, 1904.)

1906. THE MIRROR OF THE SEA: MEMORIES AND IMPRESSIONS. London: Methuen, 1906. N. Y.: Harper, 1906.
(Sections previously printed in "Pall Mall," "The Daily Mail," and "Blackwood's," 1905—1906.)

1907. THE SECRET AGENT: A SIMPLE TALE.
London: Methuen, 1907. N. Y.: Harper, 1907.
(Appeared as a serial in "Ridgeway's Weekly," October 6, 1906 to January 12, 1907.)

1908. A SET OF SIX: TALES.
London: Methuen, 1908. N. Y.: McClure, Phillips, 1908.
Contents: GASPER RUIZ, THE INFORMER, THE BRUTE, (1907), AN ANARCHIST, (1906), THE DUEL, (1908), IL CONDE, (1907).
See List of Short Stories.

1909. SOME REMINISCENCES.
Published serially in "English Review," December,
1908 to June 1909.
1912. Published by Nash, London.
1912. N. Y., Harper, under the title A PERSONAL
RECORD.

1911. UNDER WESTERN EYES: A NOVEL.
London: Methuen, 1911. N. Y.: Harper, 1911.
(Published serially in "English Review," December,
1910 to October 1911.)

1912. 'TWIXT LAND AND SEA: TALES.
London: Dent, 1912. N. Y.: Doran, 1912.
Contents: FREYA OF THE SEVEN ISLES, A SMILE
OF FORTUNE, and THE SECRET SHARER.   (1910)

1914. CHANCE: A TALE IN TWO PARTS.
London: Methuen, 1914. N. Y.: Doubleday, 1914.
(Appeared as a serial in "The New York Herald,"
January 21 to June 30, 1912.)

1915. VICTORY: AN ISLAND TALE.
London: Methuen, 1915. N. Y.: Doubleday, 1915.
(The cloth edition published by Doubleday shows on
the inside board-covering a map illustrating the
approximate scenes of Conrad's stories. The same
map is in "The Bookman" 41:128.)
This novel has been dramatized by B. Macdonald
Hastings, and presented at the Globe Theatre, London, with Miss Marie Lohr as Lena. See an un-
favorable review of the play, "Collared Conrad" by
Gilbert Cannan in "The Nation," April 5, 1919. It
has also been produced in the moving pictures.

1915. WITHIN THE TIDES: TALES.
London: Dent, 1915. N. Y.: Doubleday, 1916.
Contents: THE PLANTER OF MALATA, (1914), THE
PARTNER, (1911), THE INN OF THE TWO
WITCHES, (1913), BECAUSE OF THE DOLLARS,
(1914).
See List of Short Stories.

1917. THE SHADOW LINE: A CONFESSION.
London: Dent, 1917. N. Y.: Doubleday, 1917.
(Published serially in the "English Review," September 1916 to March 1917.)

1919. THE ARROW OF GOLD.
London: Dent, 1919. N. Y.: Doubleday, 1919.
(Published as a serial in "Lloyd's Magazine," December 1918 to February 1920.)

1920. THE RESCUE: A ROMANCE OF THE SHALLOWS.
London: Dent, 1920. N. Y.: Doubleday, 1920.
(Published as a serial in "Land and Water" [England], January 30 to July 31, 1919; and in "Romance," November, 1919 to May, 1920.

1921. NOTES ON MY BOOKS.
N. Y.: Doubleday, February, 1921.
This is a collection of Conrad's notes on the source and inception of the characters and plot of his stories. These notes are also published as prefatory matter in the Sun-Dial Edition of his works, 1921.

The complete works of Joseph Conrad are now published in uniform cloth or limp leather (The Deep Sea Limp Leather Edition) editions by Doubleday, Page & Company, Garden City, N. Y.

The Sun Dial Edition cf Conrad's collected works, in ten volumes, was published in 1921 by W. Heinemann, London, and by Doubleday, Page & Company, Garden City, N. Y. This edition is limited to 750 copies, the first volume of each set signed by the author. The twenty prefaces give Conrad's comments on the "obscure origins" of his tales.

B. *Alphabetical List of Short Stories*

AMY FOSTER
Appeared in "The Illustrated London News," December 14, 21, 28, 1901.
Published in FALK, 1903.

AN ANARCHIST
In "Harper's Monthly" 113:406, August, 1906.
Now published in A SET OF SIX, 1908.

THE ARISTOCRAT (PRINCE ROMAN)
In "The Metropolitan," January 1912, under title of THE ARISTOCRAT.
"Oxford and Cambridge Review," January 1912, under title of PRINCE ROMAN.

BECAUSE OF THE DOLLARS
Appeared under the title LAUGHING ANNE in "The Metropolitan," September, 1914.
Published in WITHIN THE TIDES, 1915.

BIG BRIERLY (from LORD JIM)
In "Living Age," 229:331, May 4, 1901.

BLACK MATE
In "London Mail," April 1908.

THE BRUTE
In "The Daily Chronicle," December 5, 1906.
In "McClure's," 30:72, November 1907. Illustrated by four pictures in color by E. L. Blumenschein.
Now published in A SET OF SIX, 1908.

IL CONDE
In "Cassell's Magazine," August, 1908.
In "The Canadian Magazine," 41:595, October, 1913.
Now published in A SET OF SIX, 1915 as IL CONDE.

THE DUEL, see A POINT OF HONOUR

THE END OF THE TETHER
In "Blackwood's" 172:1, 202, 395, 520, 685, 794, July to December, 1902.
Now published in YOUTH.

FALK
Published in FALK, 1903.

FREYA OF THE SEVEN ISLES
In "The Metropolitan," New York, April, 1912.
Published in " 'Twixt Land and Sea," 1912.

GASPAR RUIZ
In "Pall Mall Magazine," July to October, 1906.
Published in A SET OF SIX.

HEART OF DARKNESS
In "Blackwood's," 165:193, 479, 634, February to April, 1899.
In "Living Age," 225:665; 226:21, June to August, 1900.
Now published in YOUTH.

HER CAPTIVITY
In "Blackwood's," 178:325, September, 1905.

THE IDIOTS
Published in TALES OF UNREST, 1908.

THE INFORMER
In "Harper's Magazine," December, 1906.
Published in A SET OF SIX, 1908.

THE INN OF THE TWO WITCHES
In "Metropolitan," May, 1913.
In "Pall Mall," 1913.
Now published in WITHIN THE TIDES.

KARAIN: A MEMORY
In "Blackwood's," 162:630, November, 1897.
In "Living Age," 215:796, December, 1897.
Now published in TALES OF UNREST.

THE LAGOON
In "Cornhill," 75:59, January, 1897.
Now published in TALES OF UNREST.

AN OUTPOST OF PROGRESS
In "Cosmopolis," 6:609, 7:1.
Now published in TALES OF UNREST.

THE PARTNER
In "Harper's Magazine," 123:850, November, 1911.
Now pulished in WITHIN THE TIDES.

THE PLANTER OF MALATA
In "Metropolitan," June and July, 1914.
Published in WITHIN THE TIDES, 1915.

A POINT OF HONOR (THE DUEL)
In "Pall Mall Magazine," January to May, 1908.
In "The Forum," 40:89, 142, 229, 348, July to October, 1908.
Now published under the title THE DUEL in A SET OF SIX.

THE RETURN
Published in TALES OF UNREST, 1898.

THE SECRET SHARER
In "Harper's Magazine," 121:349, 530, August to September, 1910.
Now published in 'TWIXT LAND AND SEA.

A SMILE OF FORTUNE
In "The London Magazine," February, 1911.
Published in 'TWIXT LAND AND SEA, 1912.

TO-MORROW
In "Pall Mall," 27:533, August, 1902.
Now published in FALK.
Dramatized by Joseph Conrad under the title ONE DAY MORE: A PLAY IN ONE ACT. Published in "The English Review," 15:16, August, 1913.
(The foot-note states that the play was performed in 1904 by the Stage Society, and also at the Theatre de l'Oeuvre, Paris.)

YOUTH
In "Blackwood's," 164:309, September, 1898.
Now published in YOUTH.

C. *Miscellaneous Writings by Conrad*

1898. ALPHONSE DAUDET
"The Outlook," April 9, 1898. Now in NOTES ON LIFE AND LETTERS.

AN OBSERVER IN MALAY
"The Academy," April 23, 1898. Now in NOTES ON LIFE AND LETTERS.

TALES OF THE SEA
"The Outlook," June 4, 1898. Now in NOTES ON LIFE AND LETTERS.

1901. "THE INHERITORS"
Author's letter to the New York Times Supplement in regard to the book, August 24, 1901, p. 603.

1904. ANATOLE FRANCE
"The Speaker," July 16, 1904. Now in NOTES ON LIFE AND LETTERS.

GUY DE MAUPASSANT
Introduction to "Yvette and Other Stories," translated by Ada Galsworthy. Now in NOTES ON LIFE AND LETTERS.

1905. HENRY JAMES: AN APPRECIATION
"North American Review," 180:102-108, January, 1905.
Reprinted in "North American Review," 203:585, April 1916.
Now in NOTES ON LIFE AND LETTERS.

THE ART OF FICTION
"Harper's Weekly," 49 pt. 1: 690, May 1905.
Now published as the preface to THE NIGGER OF THE NARCISSUS.

BOOKS
"The Speaker," July 15, 1905.
Now in NOTES ON LIFE AND LETTERS.

AUTOCRACY AND WAR
"Fortnightly Review," o. s. 84:1, July, 1905.
"Fortnightly Review," n. s. 78:1, July, 1905.
"North American Review," 181:33-55, July, 1905.
Now in NOTES ON LIFE AND LETTERS.

1908. Review of Anatole France's L'ISLE DES PENGOUINS
       "English Review," 1:188, December, 1908.

1912. SOME REFLECTIONS ON THE LOSS OF THE
       TITANIC
       "English Review," 11:304, May 1912.
       Now in NOTES ON LIFE AND LETTERS.

       SOME ASPECTS OF THE ADMIRABLE INQUIRY
       "English Review," 11:581, July, 1912.
       Now in NOTES ON LIFE AND LETTERS.

1913. ONE DAY MORE (Dramatization of TO-MORROW)
       "English Review," 15:16, August, 1913.

1914. THE LESSON OF THE COLLISION: A MONOGRAPH
       UPON THE LOSS OF THE "EMPRESS OF INDIA"
       "The Illustrated London News," June 6, 1914.

1915. THE SHOCK OF WAR
       "Daily News," March 29, 1915.

       TO POLAND IN WAR-TIME
       "Daily News," March 31, 1915.

       THE NORTH SEA ON THE EVE OF WAR
       "Daily News," April 6, 1915.

       MY RETURN TO CRACOW
       "Daily News," April 9, 1915.
       These four papers are now published in NOTES ON
       LIFE AND LETTERS under the title of POLAND
       REVISITED.

1917. THE WARRIOR'S SOUL
       "Land and Water," March 29, 1917.

1918. MY "LORD JIM"
       Conrad's answers to the objections against his use
       of Marlow, and his account of the real Lord Jim.
       The preface to the new Sun-Dial edition of LORD
       JIM. "Bookman," 46:539, January, 1918.

"MR. CONRAD IS NOT A JEW"
A letter by Conrad repudiating the statement that
he is a Jew, and asserting that he is a Roman
Catholic.
"The New Republic," 16:109, August 24, 1918.

"WELL DONE"
"Daily Mail," August 22, 23, 24, 1918.
Now in NOTES ON LIFE AND LETTERS.

THE FIRST NEWS
"Reveille," No. I, August, 1918.
Now in NOTES ON LIFE AND LETTERS.

TRADITION
"Daily Mail," March 18, 1918.
Now in NOTES ON LIFE AND LETTERS.

1919. POLAND: THE CRIME OF PARTITION
"Fortnightly Review," 111:657-669, May, 1919.
Now published under the title of THE CRIME OF
PARTITION in NOTES ON LIFE AND LETTERS.

CONFIDENCE
"Daily Mail," June 30, 1919.
Now in NOTES ON LIFE AND LETTERS.

STEPHEN CRANE: A NOTE WITHOUT DATES
"London Mercury," 1:192, December, 1919.
"Bookman," 50:529-31, February, 1920.
Now in NOTES ON LIFE AND LETTERS.

1920. ON POLAND
"The New York Tribune," April 5, 1920.

THREE CONRAD NOVELS
"Dial," 69: 619-630, December, 1920.
Now published as prefaces to the three novels: AN
OUTCAST OF THE ISLANDS, LORD JIM, NOS-
TROMO in the Sun-Dial Collected Edition.

1921. FIVE PREFACES
"London Mercury," 3:493-509, March, 1921.

III. CRITICISMS OF CONRAD

A. *Books on Conrad*

1914. JOSEPH CONRAD: A STUDY

By Richard Curle. Doubleday, Page & Company, 1914.
(This appeared first in part as articles in "The Bookman," July to October, 1914, 30:662 and 40:99, 187.)

This is the first complete book written solely to criti-
cize and estimate Conrad's work, and it still remains
the longest appreciation that has appeared. Mr.
Curle explains the reasons for Conrad's unpopularity
with the majority of the reading public, then proceeds to analyze his greatness. The biographical
sketch is of the briefest in order that more space
may be given to actual criticism of his work. The
second chapter is given over to elementary synopses
of each of Conrad's novels and stories—"spade work"
for the uninitiated, Mr. Curle calls it. There is also
a bibliography.

1915. JOSEPH CONRAD: A SHORT STUDY

By Wilson Follett. Privately printed by Doubleday,
Page & Company, 1915.

This small volume is one of the best criticisms of
Conrad yet written. It is a scholarly critique of the
purpose, philosophy, style, and method of Conrad.
Mr. Follett's style is not barrenly lucid, but it is
always distinguished.

1915. JOSEPH CONRAD

By Hugh Walpole. London, Nisbet & Company, Ltd.,
1915. N. Y., Holt, 1915.

Contains English and American bibliographies of
Conrad's novels.

This, the shortest book about Conrad, is one of the
most sympathetic appreciations. After giving a
short biographical account of Conrad as a necessary
prologue to an understanding of his work, Mr.
Walpole discusses him as Novelist, (that is, as to
the Theme, as to the Form, as to the Creation of
character), as Poet, and as Romanticist and Realist.

B. *Articles about Conrad*

First List

1904. Clifford, Hugh. THE GENIUS OF MR. JOSEPH CONRAD. "North American Review," 178:842, June, 1904.

This is one of the most sympathetic of the early reviews.

1917. Follet, H. F. and W. Follett. CONTEMPORARY NOVELISTS—JOSEPH CONRAD. "The Atlantic," 119:233-43, February, 1917.

This is based to some extent on Wilson Follett's book on Conrad. It asserts that the realism of Conrad is due to his understanding of the "tragic unfitness of things," especially as revealed in those souls cut off by barriers of race, of spirit, of accident. It is a discussion, also, of Conrad's technique, and of his philosophy.

1908. Galsworthy, John. JOSEPH CONRAD: A DISQUISITION. "Fortnightly Review" o. s. 89:627-633, April, 1908. "Fortnightly Review" n. s. 83:627. "Living Age," 257: 416, May 16, 1908.

This is one of the first and finest appreciations of Conrad. Galsworthy discusses the "certain cosmic spirit" of Conrad's art, and his method of expressing that spirit, and concludes with an ironic explanation of his lack of popularity. This article through its critical enthusiasm did much to win recognition for Conrad.

1911. Hueffer, Ford Madox. THE GENIUS OF JOSEPH CONRAD. "English Review," 10:66-83, December, 1911.

This is a sympathetic and very enthusiastic appreciation of Conrad's art by his fellow novelist and collaborator. Hueffer acclaims Conrad "the finest of the Elizabethans." This article is especially illuminating in regard to Conrad's method. Hueffer used italicized words in paragraphs from ROMANCE to show that the descriptive phrases are his, the words of action, Conrad's—contrary to the belief of most critics. Conrad's method, he says, is: "Never state: present. Never comment: state."

1918. Robertson, J. M. (M.P.). THE NOVELS OF JOSEPH CONRAD. "North American Review," 208: 439-53, September, 1918.

This is one of the latest good appreciations of Conrad. After a comparison of Meredith and Conrad, Mr. Robertson proceeds to a discussion of Conrad's method of plot development, of character creation, of treatment of atmosphere, and of his realism and idealism.

1915. Symons, Arthur. CONRAD. "Forum," 53:579-592, May, 1915.

(A review of this article is in "Current Opinion," January, 1918.)

Symons cannot be disregarded as a critic. Nevertheless, his article, though thoroughly appreciative of Conrad's genius, leaves the impression that Conrad is more than anything else a cynic. Symons discusses both his philosophy and his technique.

1918. de Voisins, Gilbert. JOSEPH CONRAD: MEMOIRE. "Revue de Paris," pt. 2:5-16, March 1, 1918.

This critic insists that Conrad is a romancer, not a realist, and admires him especially for his creation of atmosphere. He criticises several books in detail.

1918. Follett, Helen Thomas and Wilson. SOME MODERN NOVELISTS: APPRECIATIONS AND ESTIMATES, NO. XII, JOSEPH CONRAD.

This is the article that appeared in "The Atlantic," February, 1917, somewhat enlarged.

1920. Hueffer, Ford Madox. THUS TO REVISIT. "English Review," 31:5. "The Dial," 69:52-60, 132- 141, 239-246, July, August, September, 1920.

This is a reminiscence by Mr. Hueffer of his collaboration with Conrad. It contains a revealing discussion of Conrad's methods.

Second List

1912. Björkman, E. JOSEPH CONRAD: MASTER OF LITERARY COLOR. (With portrait and bibliography to 1912.) "Review of Reviews," 445: 557, May, 1912. Reprinted in VOICES OF TOMORROW by the same author under heading "General Knights of Modern Literature." M. Kennerly, pub., 1913.

This is an excellent summary of the life of Conrad, and analysis of his style. Björkman objects to Galsworthy's statement that to Conrad "nature is first, man second."

1902. Clifford, Hugh. THE ART OF MR. JOSEPH CONRAD. "Spectator," 89:827, November 29, 1902. "Living Age," 236:120, January 10, 1903.

This is really a book review of YOUTH. It is devoted primarily to a discussion of Conrad's power of description.

1914. Colbron, Grace Isabel. JOSEPH CONRAD'S WOMEN. "Bookman," 38:476, January, 1914.

This is a discussion of the psychology of Conrad's women, and of the subordinate place they take in his stories.

1916. Donlin, George Barnard. THE ART OF JOSEPH CONRAD. "Dial," 61:172, September 21, 1916.

This is really an explanation of the limited circle of Conrad's readers through a discussion of his method, his irony, his philosophy, his style.

1914. Huneker, James. THE GENIUS OF JOSEPH CONRAD. "North American," 200:270-179, August, 1914. Reprinted in IVORY APES AND PEACOCKS, Scribner's, 1915.

This is an appreciation of Conrad as an artist. In these days "Joseph Conrad stands solitary among English novelists as the ideal of a pure and disinterested artist."

1914. James, Henry. THE NEW NOVEL, 1914. NOTES ON NOVELISTS, p. 345-353. C. Scribner's Sons.

This is essentially a discussion of Conrad's method as revealed in CHANCE. It is unfortunately written in Mr. James's most tortuous style.

1917. Mencken, H. L. JOSEPH CONRAD. In A BOOK OF PREFACES. A. A. Knopf, 1917.

This is a continuous spluttering of an apparent misogynist. Mr. Mencken likes Conrad because he makes him out to be the same kind of cynic as himself. There is some wheat in much chaff. The article contains an entertaining criticism of the criticisms of Conrad.

1918. Pease, Frank. JOSEPH CONRAD. "Nation," 107:510-13, November 2, 1918.

This is a short but well-written and individual discussion of the new type of adventure found in Conrad's novels and tales. Conrad, Mr. Pease thinks, has "remade adventure."

1916. Phelps, William Lyon. THE ADVANCE OF THE ENGLISH NOVEL. Published N. Y., Dodd, Mead & Co., 1916. On Conrad, Chapter VIII, pp. 192-209. (Originally appeared as a series of articles in "Bookman," 42:297, May 1916.)

This is a criticism in Mr. Phelps' usual entertaining style of the work of Conrad as an artist. After a brief resumé of the life of Conrad, Mr. Phelps discusses his style, his method, and his individual books, and incidentally compares Conrad with other writers, notably Stevenson.

1912. Reynolds, Stephen. JOSEPH CONRAD AND SEA FICTION. "Quarterly Review," 217: 159-180, July, 1912. "Living Age," 276:264, February, 1913.

This is primarily an appreciation of Conrad's criticism of life and character as revealed in his novels of the sea. Other books, however, are also included in the discussion.

1916. Freeman, John. THE MODERNS, pp. 243-264. London, R. Scott, 1916.

1919. Hall, Leland. JOSEPH CONRAD. Chapter IX, pp. 161-179 in ENGLISH LITERATURE DURING THE LAST HALF CENTURY, by J. W. Cuniffe, N. Y. Macmillan Co., 1919.

1919. Moore, Edward. A NOTE ON MR. CONRAD. "New Statesman," 13: 590-2, September 13, 1919. "Living Age," 304:101-4, January 10, 1920. "Current Opinion," 67:320-1, December, 1919. (Condensed, with an excellent photograph of Conrad.)

This is an interesting discussion of Conrad as a skeptic, and as a psychologist who sees the men and women he has created not as living souls, but as mere laboratory specimens of humanity.

1920. Gwynn, Stephen. NOVELS OF JOSEPH CONRAD. "Edinburgh Review," 231:318-19, April, 1920.

This is an analysis of fifteen of Conrad's books, including a brief discussion of his method and philosophy.

1921. Jean, Aubry, G. JOSEPH CONRAD'S CONFESSIONS. "Fortnightly Review," 115:782-90, May, 1921.

This is a discussion of Conrad's attitude toward his own creative writing and toward life, under phase of a review of the "Author's Notes" printed as prefaces to the collected edition.

Third List

1914. Boynton, H. W. JOSEPH CONRAD. "The Nation," 98:395-7, April 9, 1914.

This is the usual type of article, summarizing briefly Conrad's life, and then proceeding to analyze the "esteem" in which he is coming to be held, through a discussion of his subjects, his method, his style, and his philosophy.

1912. Cooper, Frederick Tabor. REPRESENTATIVE ENGLISH STORY TELLERS: JOSEPH CONRAD. "The Bookman," 35:61-70, March, 1912.

This is a discussion of (1) the methods of Conrad, and (2) of his works. It begins as an answer to Galsworthy's statement in his article that Conrad has the "cosmic spirit," that is, that the Universe is always saying, "The little part called man is always smaller than the whole." Mr. Cooper insists that the "vital and tremendous human interest" in Conrad's books is their most essential spirit.

1915. Curle, Richard. JOSEPH CONRAD AND VICTORY. "Fortnightly Review," 104:670 October, 1915.

This is a book review of "Victory," contrasting it primarily in regard to method, with "Chance," and proceeding to a discussion of the stages in the evolution of Conrad's method as seen in his other works.

1911. Curran, E. F. A MASTER OF LANGUAGE. "The Catholic World, 92:769-805, March, 1911.

This long appreciation of Conrad is full of enthusiastic but uncritical estimates of characters and books. The author's orthodox Roman Catholicism unexpectedly and naively colors his remarks.

1918. Cutler, Frances Wentworth. WHY MARLOW? "Sewanee Review," 26: 28, January, 1918.

This is an analysis of the purpose of Marlow in Conrad's method of presenting his stories.

1919. Gerould,   Katherine   Fullerton.   EIDOLONS   OF
       ULYSSES. "The Bookman," 49:368, May, 1919.
       This is an enthusiastic review of "The Arrow of Gold."
       Mrs. Gerould ranks Conrad with the greatest creative
       writers of the world.

1906. Macy, John Albert. JOSEPH CONRAD. "The Atlantic
       Monthly," 98:697-702, November, 1906.
       This is the earliest "Atlantic" recognition of Conrad.
       The author is evidently puzzled by Conrad's origin-
       ality, which he recognizes, but which he cannot re-
       frain from disparaging.   However, he grants that
       Conrad is "really important," especially as a "fine
       writer of sentences."

1917. Macy, John. KIPLING AND CONRAD. "The Dial,"
       62:441, May 17, 1917.
       This is a review of THE SHADOW LINE with empha-
       sis on Conrad's descriptive power.

1919. Dargan, E. Preston. THE VOYAGES OF CONRAD.
       "The Dial," 66:638-41, June 28, 1919.
       This is a somewhat superficial review of Conrad's
       work to 1919.

1919. Reilly, Joseph. THE SHORT STORIES OF JOSEPH
       CONRAD. "Catholic World," 109:163-75, May, 1919.
       Mr. Reilly discusses Conrad's use of setting, and the
       reality of his characters; also his philosophy of life
       as revealing his Slavic temperament.

1920. Seldes, Gilbert. A NOVELIST OF COURAGE. "The
       Dial," 69:52, 132, August, 1920.
       This is a review of THE RESCUE with a brief dis-
       cussion of Conrad's style.

1920. Bellesor, A. LE PREMIER ROMAN DE CONRAD:
       LA FOLIE ALMAYER. "Revue Politique et Litter-
       aire" (Revue Bleue), 58:599-603, October, 1920.

1921. McFee, William. THE SEA—AND CONRAD. "Book-
       man," 53:102-8, April, 1921.
       This is a reminiscent commentary of the effect of read-
       ing Conrad on different types of people, especially
       on seamen.

IV. BOOK REVIEWS

(Partial List Only)

ALMAYER'S FOLLY
> Academy, 47:502, 1895.
> Athenaeum, 1895, pt. 1, 671.
> Bookman, 2:39, August, 1895.

AN OUTCAST OF THE ISLANDS
> Academy, 49:525, June 27, 1896.
> Athenaeum, 1896, pt. 2:91, July 18, 1896.
> Bookman, 4:166, October, 1896.
> N. Y. Times, 1896, September 23, p. 10.
> Saturday Review, 81:509, May 1916.

THE ARROW OF GOLD
> Athenaeum, p. 720, August 8, 1919.
> Bookman, 49:368, May, 1919. (K. F. Gerould)
> Boston Transcript, p. 8, April 20, 1919.
> Boston Transcript, p. 11, May 24, 1919.
> Nation, 108:951, June 14, 1919.
> New Republic, 19:56, May 10, 1919.
> N. Y. Times, 24:189, April 13, 1919.
> Outlook, 122:122, May 21, 1919.
> Publishers' Weekly, 95:1129, April 19, 1919. (F. T. Cooper)
> Living Age, 302:792-5, September 27, 1919. (S. Colvin)
> Deux Mondes, 6 per 53:676-85, Octobre 1, 1919. (L. Gillet)
> Saturday Review, 128:179, August 23, 1919.
> Spectator, 122:410, September 27, 1919.
> The Times, London, Literary Supplement, p. 422, August 7, 1919.

CHANCE
> Academy, 86:145, January 31, 1914.   (F. T. Cooper)
> Atlantic, 114:530, October, 1914.
> Athenaeum, 1914, 1:88, January 17, 1914.
> Bookman, 39:323, May, 1914.
> Boston Transcript, p. 9, January 31, 1914.
> Boston Transcript, p. 8, March 21, 1914.
> Independent, 78:173, April 27, 1914.
> Literary Digest, 48:1119, May 9, 1914.
> Nation, 98:396, April 9, 1914.
> N. Y. Times, 19:396, April 9, 1914.

Outlook, 107:45, May 2, 1914.
Publishers' Weekly, 85: 1335, April 18, 1914.
Review of Reviews, 49: 373, March 1914.
Saturday Review, 117:117, January 24, 1914.
Spectator, 112:101, January 17, 1914.
Springfield Republican, p. 5, April 16, 1914.

FALK

Bookman, 18:311, November 1, 1903. (F. T. Cooper)
N. Y. Times Supplement, 1903, October 24, p. 756.
N. Y. Tribune Supplement, 1903, September 27, p. 11.
Academy, 64:463, May 9, 1903.

THE INHERITORS

Academy, 61:93, August 3, 1901.
Athenaeum, 1901, pt. 2, p. 151, August 3, 1901.
N. Y. Times Supplement, 1901, July 13, p. 499.
N. Y. Times Supplement, 1901, August 24. (By Conrad
himself)

LORD JIM

Academy, 59:443, November 10, 1900.
Athenaeum, 1900 pt. 2:576, November 3, 1900.
Bookman, 13:187, April, 1901.
Current Literature, 30:222, February, 1901.
N. Y. Times Supplement, 1900, November 10, p. 770.
N. Y. Times Supplement, 1900, December 1, pp. 836, 839.
N. Y. Tribune Supplement, 1900, November 3, p. 10.
Speaker, n. s., 3, 215.

THE MIRROR OF THE SEA

Literary Digest, 33:685, November 10, 1906.
The Times, London, 5:344, October 12, 1906.
Nation, 83:374, November 1, 1906.
Outlook, 84:678, November 17, 1906.
Academy, 71:393, October 20, 1906.
Athenaeum, 1906, pt. 2:513, October 27, 1906.
Spectator, 97:889, December 1, 1906.
N. Y. Times, Supplement, 1906, November 10, p. 734.
Outlook (London), 18:480.

THE NIGGER OF THE NARCISSUS

Academy, 53:163, February 5, 1898.
Bookman, 8:91, October, 1898.
Bookman, 39:563, July, 1914.

Book Buyer, 16:350, May, 1898.
Illustrated London News, 112:50 & 172.
Nation, 67:53.
N. Y. Times Supplement, 1898, May 21, p. 344.
N. Y. Tribune Supplement, 1898, April 3, p. 17,.
Pall Mall Magazine, 14:428.
Speaker, 17:83.

NOSTROMO

Atlantic, 97:45, January, 1906.
Athenaeum, 1904, p. 2; 619, November 5, 1904.
Bookman, 20:217, November, 1904. (F. T. Cooper)
Dial, 38:126, February 16, 1905.
Critic, 46:377.
Independent, 58:557.
N. Y. Times Supplement, 1904, October 29, p. 735 and
   December 31, p. 944.
Spectator, 93:800.
Reader, 5:618, April, 1905.

NOTES ON LIFE AND LETTERS

N. Y. Times, p. 10, May 8, 1921.
The Times, London, Literary Supplement, p. 141, March
   3, 1921.
The New Statesman, 16:674. (Robert Lynd)
Living Age, 309:221-4, April 23, 1921. (Reprint of R.
   Lynd's article.)
Current Opinion, 70:819-21, June, 1921.
New Republic, vol. 27:25, June 1, 1921.

NOTES ON MY BOOKS

Fortnightly Review, May, 1921, pp. 782-790. ("Joseph
   Conrad's Confessions," by G. Jean-Aubry.)

A PERSONAL RECORD (SOME REMINISCENCES)

Athenaeum, 1912, 1:124, February 3.
Bookman, London, 42:26, April, 1912.
Catholic World, 95:254, May, 1912.
Dial, 52:172, March 1, 1912.
Independent, 72:678, March 28, 1912.
Nation, 94:238, March 7, 1912.
N. Y. Times, 17:77, February 18, 1912.
North American, 195: 569, April, 1912.
Spectator, 109:60, July 13, 1912.

THE RESCUE

Athenaeum, p. 15, July 2, 1920.
Booklist, 16:346, July 1920.
Boston Transcript, p. 4, May 26, 1920.
Catholic World, 112:394, December, 1920.
Dial, 69:191, August, 1920. (Gilbert Seldes)
Freeman, 1:454, July, 1920.
Nation, 110:804, June 12, 1920.
N. Y. Times, 25:263, May 23, 1920.
Outlook, 125:280, June 9, 1920.
Weekly Review, 2:604, June 5, 1920.
Weekly Review, 2:629, June 16, 1920.
Spectator, 124:52, July 10, 1920.
The Times, London, Literary Supplement, p. 419, July 1, 1920.
Wisconsin Library Bulletin, 16:193, November, 1920.

ROMANCE

Academy, 65:469, October 31, 1903.
Athenaeum, 1903, pt. 2:610, November 7, 1903.
Dial, 37:37, July 16, 1904.
Bookman, 20:544.
N. Y. Times Supplement, 1904, May 14, p. 325.
Outlook, N. Y., 77:424-5.

THE SECRET AGENT

Academy, 74:413, February 1, 1908.
Athenaeum, 1907, pt. 2:361, September 28, 1907.
Albany Review, London, 2:229.
Bookman, 26:531, January, 1908. (Stewart Edward White)
Bookman, 26:669, February, 1908.   (F. T. Cooper)
Current Literature, 44:223, February, 1908.
Dial, 43:252, October 16, 1907.
Independent, 64:105, January 9, 1908.
Nation, 85: 285, September 26, 1907.
N. Y. Times, 12:562, September 21, 1907.
N. Y. Times, 12:655, October 19, 1907.
Outlook, London, 20:652.
Outlook, N. Y., 87:309, October 13, 1907.
Putnam's, 3:370, December, 1907.
Spectator, 99:400, September 21, 1907.
The Times, London, 6:285, September 20, 1907.

A SET OF SIX

Athenaeum, 1908, pt. 2:237, August 29, 1908.
Boston Transcript, p. 6, January 23, 1915.
Catholic World, 100:825, March, 1915.
Nation, 100:199, February 18, 1915.
N. Y. Times, 20:38, January 31, 1915.
Outlook, London, 22:246.
Publishers' Weekly, 87:480, February, 13, 1915.
Spectator, 101:237, August 15, 1908.
Springfield Republican, p. 5, April 1, 1915.

THE SHADOW LINE

Athenaeum, p. 253, May, 1917.
Bookman, 45:536, July, 1917.
Boston Transcript, p. 6, May 5, 1917.
Dial, 62:442, May, 1917. (John Macy)
Independent, 90:437, June 2, 1917.
Literary Digest, 55:36, October 27, 1917.
Nation, 104:760, June 28, 1917. (H. W. Boynton)
Nation, 105:600, November 29, 1917.
New Republic, 11:194, June 16, 1917.
N. Y. Times, 22:157, April 22, 1917.
North American, 205:949, June, 1917.
Outlook, 116:116, May 16, 1917.
Review of Reviews, 55:663, June, 1917.
Saturday Review, 123:281, March 24, 1917.
Spectator, 118:391, March 31, 1917.
Springfield Republican, p. 19, May 27, 1917.
The Times, London, Literary Supplement, p. 138, March 22, 1917.

TALES OF UNREST

Academy, 56:66, January, 1899.
Athenaeum, 1898, pt. 1:564, April 30, 1898.
Nation, 67:54, July 21, 1898.
Book Buyer, 16:350, May, 1918.
Literary World, London, 57:534.
N. Y. Tribune Supplement, 1898, April 3, p. 17.
Spectator, 109:815-6, November 16, 1912.

'TWIXT LAND AND SEA

Athenaeum, 1912, 2:446, October 19.
Bookman, 37:85, March, 1913.
Boston Transcript, p. 22, January 29, 1913.

Independent, 74:538, March 6, 1913.
Nation, 96:360, April 10, 1913.
N. Y. Times, 18:51, February 2, 1913.
Outlook, 103:596, March 16, 1913.
Review of Reviews, 47:762, June, 1913.
Saturday Review, 114:492, October 19, 1912.
Spectator, 109:815, November 16, 1912.
Springfield Republican, p.5, February 20, 1913.

TYPHOON

Academy, 64:463, May 9, 1903.
Athenaeum, 1903, pt. 1:558, May 2, 1903.
Forum, 34:400, January, 1903.
Harper's Weekly, 46:412, October 4, 1902.
N. Y. Times Supplement, 1902, September 20, p. 626.
N. Y. Tribune Supplement, 1902, September 14, p. 12.

UNDER WESTERN EYES

Athenaeum, 1911, 2:183, October 21.
Bookman, 34:411, December, 1911.
Current Literature, 52:236, February, 1912.
N. Y. Times Supplement, 16:818, December 10, 1911.
North American, 194:935, December, 1911.
Saturday Review, 112:495, October 14, 1911.

VICTORY

Athenaeum, 1915, 2:208, September 25.
Atlantic, 116:511, October, 1915.
Bookman, 41:322, May, 1915. (Grace I. Colborn.)
Boston Transcript, p. 24, March 24, 1915.
Current Opinion, 58:351, May, 1915.
Dial, 58:383, May 13, 1915.
Fortnightly, o. s. 104:670, October, 1915 (n. s. 98:670.)
    (Richard Curle)
Literary Digest, 50:885, April 17, 1915.
Nation, 100:416, April 15, 1915.
New Republic, 2:sup. 6, April 17, 1915.
N. Y. Times, 20:109, March 28, 1915.
Outlook, 110:44, May 5, 1915.
Publishers' Weekly, 87:924, March 20, 1915.
Review of Reviews, 51:761, June, 1915.
Saturday Review, 120:298, September 25, 1915.
Springfield Republican, p. 5, May 13, 1915.

WITHIN THE TIDES

Athenaeum, 1915, 1:211, March 6.
Boston Transcript, p. 6, January 22, 1916.
Dial, 60:216, March 2, 1916.
Independent, 86:73, April 1ô, 1916.
Nation, 102:164, February 10, 1916.
N. Y. Times, 21:17, January 16, 1916.
Publishers' Weekly, 89:642, February 19, 1916.
Review of Reviews, 53:377, March, 1916.
Saturday Review, 119:311, March 20, 1915.
Spectator, 114:338, March 6, 1915.
Springfield Republican, p. 15, February 20, 1916.

YOUTH

Academy, 63:606, December 6, 1902.
Athenaeum, 1902, pt. 2:824, December 20, 1902.
Nation, N. Y., 76:478, June 11, 1903.
N. Y. Times Supplement, 1902, December 13, p. 898.
N. Y. Times Supplement, 1903, April 4, p. 224.
Speaker, n. s., 7:442. (John Masefield)
Spectator, 89:827, 1902. (H. Clifford)
Critic, September, 1903.

As individual stories:

N. Y. Times Supplement, 1899, June 17, p. 385.
N. Y. Times Supplement, 1900, March 3, p. 138.
N. Y. Times Supplement, 1898, September 18, p. 12.

V. MISCELLANEOUS

A. *Brief Articles on the Personality of Conrad*

1904. "The Personality of Conrad."
Academy, 66:198, February 20, 1904.

1904. Photograph of Conrad's home "Pent Farm," and brief comment. Bookman, 19:449, July, 1904.

1904. Comment on his collaboration with Ford Madox Hueffer. Bookman, 19:544, August, 1904.

1913. How "Almayer's Folly" was written (With small photographs of his wife and son, and of his home.) Bookman, 38:352, December, 1913.

1914. "A Sermon in One Man" by Mary Austin. Harper's Weekly, 58, pt. 2:20, May 16, 1914.

1915. Picture of the "Otago," Conrad's first ship, and also a map illustrating the world of his novels and tales. Bookman, 41:129, April, 1915.

1918. An Account of how Conrad was isolated in Poland at the outbreak of the war. Bookman, 46:659, February, 1918.

1920. "Conrad in Cracow" (Illustrated) Outlook, 124: 382-3, March 3, 1920.

1920. "Joseph Conrad, Sexagenarian," by E. P. Bendz. English Studies, 51:391-406.

B. *Poems to Conrad*

1908. "Old Ships" by F. Maurice. Spectator, 101:734, November 7, 1908.

1917. "Conrad in Snap-Shots of English Authors" by Richard Butler Glaezner. Bookman, 45:346, June, 1917.

C. *Portraits of Conrad*

1898. Book Buyer, 16:389, June, 1898.

1898. Academy, 55:82, October 15, 1898.

1903. Review of Reviews, 27:630, May, 1903.

1908. Independent, 65:1066, November 5, 1908.

1911. English Review, 9:476, October, 1911.
         Pencil drawing by Will Rothenstein.

1912. Current Literature, 52:470, April, 1912.

1913. Bookman, 37:557, May, 1912.

1914. Review of Reviews, 49:373, March 1914.

1914. Current Opinion, 56:374, May, 1914.

1915. Current Opinion, 58:351, May, 1915.

1915. Review of Reviews, 51:761, June, 1915.

1917. Bookman, 45:637, August, 1917.
         (Photograph of the bust of Conrad by Jo Davidson.)

1918. Bookman, 46:658, February, 1918.
         (Photograph taken in Poland, October, 1914.)

1919. Current Opinion, 67:320-1, December, 1919.

1920. Outlook, 124:382-3, March 3, 1920.

1920. World's Work, 39:495, March, 1920.

1921. Current Opinion, 70:819-21, June, 1921.

1921. World's Work, 42:189, June, 1921.

VI. ROMANTICISM AND REALISM

A.   *A Brief Summary of the Critical Definitions of*
Romanticism and Realism.

A resumé of the best known critical definitions of
Romanticism and Realism will establish the fact that the
distinctions between the two have been variously emphasized as differences in subject matter, in method, in spirit
and purpose of the author; but no one literary definition
has yet been formulated to comprehend all three phases.
(See supra, page 5, ff.)

In his *History of English Romanticism in the Eighteenth Century,* Henry Beers devotes the whole of the
long first chapter to a summary of all preceding definitions of Romanticism.   He strikes off as his own rough,
working definition: "Romanticism, then, means the repro-
duction in modern art of the life and thought of the
Middle Ages."   Georg Brandes says, "At first Romanticism was, in its essence, merely a spirited defence of
localization in literature," and Walter Raleigh draws the
same general conclusion: "Romance, in its modern development, is largely a question of background.   A
romantic love-affair might be defined as a love-affair in
other than domestic surroundings."   The briefest summary of all historical definflitions of this term is given
by Neilsen in *Essentials of Poetry*:

> "Among the host of definitions that have been
> offered there are three that have been especially per-
> sistent.   Heine, speaking of the Romantic school in
> Germany, finds the heart of the movement in the
> return to the Middle Ages.   French critics have laid
> especial stress on the growth of the subjective ele-
> ment, and speak of the 'rediscovery of the soul' and
> the 'rebirth of the spiritual.'   In England the favorite

phrase has been 'the return to Nature,' with a special reference to the increased prominence in the poetry of the time, of direct description of external beauty."

Mr. Neilsen's own definition he states in the following words:

> "There are three fundamental elements in poetry: imagination, reason, and the sense of fact . . . Romanticism is the tendency characterized by the predominance of reason over imagination and the sense of fact. Realism is the tendency characterized by the predominance of the sense of fact over imagination and reason."
>
> "Emotion, or intensity, does not belong, as a special possession, to one class or school, but is a general source of poetic reality in all."

"No single formula can hope to describe and distinguish two eras or define two tempers of mind," says Raleigh. "If I had to choose a single characteristic of Romance as the most noteworthy, I think I should choose Distance, and should call Romance the Magic of Distance."

We are all familiar with Pater's famous phrase that Romance implies "the addition of strangeness to beauty, of curiosity to desire."

It is Mr. Woodberry who gives the essence of this Romantic spirit when he says, "Romantic art is touched with mystery, it has richness and intricacy of form not fully comprehended, it suggests more than it satisfies, it stirs an unconfined and wandering emotion, it invigorates an adventurous will."

The most famous definition of Realism is given by Emile Zola, the greatest of the Naturalists, in his essays on *The Experimental Novel*. Zola uses the terms Realism and Naturalism as synonyms. He says: "To give your reader a scrap of human life, that is the whole purpose of the naturalistic novel." And again:

"And this is what constitutes the experimental
novel: to possess a knowledge of the mechanism of
the phenomena inherent in man, to show the machin-
ery of his intellectual and sensory manifestations,
under the influence of heredity and environment,
such as physiology shall give them to us, and then
finally to exhibit man living in social conditions produced by himself, which he modifies daily, and in the
heart of whicn he himself experiences a continual
manifestation."

"Experimental science," Zola says in discussing the experimental novelist, "has no necessity to worry about the
'why' of things; it simply explains the 'how'."

William Dean Howells has put it in its simplest form:
"Realism is nothing more and nothing less than the truth-
ful treatment of material." The qualifications and aims
of the writer of the realistic novel M. Reynier gives as
follows:

"Ce que l'on croit pouvoir exiger d'un romancier
réaliste: le don de découvrir dans la masse des dé-
tails les traits distinctifs et prédominants; cette
sincérité du véritable observateur qui se soumet abso-
lument à son objet; cette curiosité universelle qui se
porte sur la variété des hommes, cette large et libér-
ale sympathie qui les considère tous comme digne
d'attention et qui, si elle a des préférences, n'en a que
pour ceux qui sont le plus près de la nature; l'art
enfin de dégager un individu de la foule, en traduisant
en faits visibles ce qu'il y a en lui d'original et
d'unique, de le montrer dans son milieu normal, dans
son temps et de peindre en lui un peu de ce milieu
et de ce temps, de le faire ainsi tout à la fois très
particulier et pourtant représentif: de telles qualités
ne peuvent évidemment se trouver réunies que chez
un fort petit nombre d'écrivains privilégiés, à une
époque de culture déjà avancée."

Robert Louis Stevenson insists that the distinction
between Romanticism and Realism is a distinction wholly

of method. "All representative art, which can be said to live," he says in *A Note on Realism,*

> "is both realistic and ideal; and the realism about which we quarrel is a matter purely of externals . . . This question of realism, let it be then clearly understood, regards not in the least the fundamental truth, but only the technical method, of a work of art."

And again in a letter discussing this same essay he becomes even more emphatic:

> "Realism I regard as a mere question of method. . . . Real art, whether ideal or realistic, addresses precisely the same feeling, and seeks the same qualities—significance or charm. And the same—the very same—inspiration is only methodically differentiated according as the artist is an arrant realist or an arrant idealist. Each, by his own method, seeks to save and perpetuate the same significance or charm; the one by suppressing, the other by forcing detail . . . I want you to help me to get people to understand that realism is a method, and only methodic in its consequences; when the realist is an artist, that is, and supposing the idealist with whom you compare him to be anything but a "farceur" and a dilettanté. The two schools of working do, and should, lead to the choice of different subjects. But that is a consequence, not a cause."

For other definitions and discussions of Romanticism and Realism consult the works listed in the bibliography in Appendix VI, B.

B.   *On Romanticism and Realism*

Henry A. Beers: A History of English Romanticism in the Eighteenth Century (1899).

Georg Brandes: Main Currents in Nineteenth Century Literature, Vols. IV and V. (1906).

Ferdinand Brunetière: Le Roman Naturaliste (1893).

E. Preston Durgan: Studies in Balzac, II.   Critical Analysis of Realism, in "Modern Philology," November, 1918.

Guy de Maupassant: Preface to "Pierre et Jean" (1894)

Clayton Hamilton: The Art of Fiction, Chapter II.   (1918)

William Dean Howells: Criticism and Fiction (1891).

Henry James: The Art of Fiction (1888).

Paul Lenoir: Histoire du Réalisme et du Naturalisme (1889).

Brander Matthews: The Historical Novel: Romance against Romanticism (1901).

William A. Neilsen: Essentials of Poetry (1912).

Bliss Perry: A Study of Prose Fiction, Chapters IX, and X. (1902)

Walter Raleigh: Romance (1915).

Gustave Reynier: Les Origines du Roman Réaliste: Introduction (1912).

Ernest Rhys: Romance (1913).

Robert Louis Stevenson: A Gossip on Romance (1895).
A Note on Realism (1883).
Victor Hugo's Romances (1895).
Letters, Vol. I.

Daniel Greenleaf Thompson: The Philosophy of Fiction in Literature, Chapter VI. (1890).

Arthur Waugh: The New Realism, "Fortnightly Review," 105:849, (May, 1916).

George Woodberry: Heart of Man: A New Defense of Poetry (1899).

C. H. Conrad Wright: A History of French Literature, Chapter XIII.   (1912)

Emile Zola: Le Roman Expérimental (1893).